Praise For <u>Dear Teacher</u>

"This book is a heartfelt cry and a warning alarm to all teachers and professional help-ers about the pain and suffering of children at home and in school. We would prefer not to hear let alone deal with this abuse. Yet who will intervene if we do not? It is my hope that John Seryak's collected first-hand accounts and commentary will heighten our sensitivity and give us courage to confront this growing problem more effectively for the sake of children everywhere."

Rev. Richard D. Clewell, D.Min.
Licensed Professional Clinical Counselor

"<u>Dear Teacher</u> is a poignant reminder to every person in authority over children as to the vital importance of their action or inaction. The consequences to a child can be life long. This book is a must read for every educator and all people concerned about the health and welfare of children."

Claire R. Reeves, President/Founder
Mothers Against Sexual Abuse, MASA

"My heart is filled so many emotions… <u>Dear Teacher</u> reinforces the difference a teacher can make in the life of a child. Each letter emphasizes how critical it is that educators are aware of the signs of abuse and understand how to interact with students who are victims of abuse and neglect. We all have a professional and moral responsibility to our children——we are their only hope and they are our only hope for a more caring and peaceful world."

Annette Kratcoski, Ph.D.
Coordinator, Curriculum & Instruction
Summit County Educational Service Center; Akron, Ohio.

"Recruiting victims of childhood abuse and neglect who can now articulate their or-deals is a great idea. They can tell us what to look for to see that a child is in pain. This is the type of practical work that is potentially very helpful to those teachers who want to go beyond the curriculum."

Douglas G. Cole, Ph.D.
Psychological Counselor

DEAR TEACHER

"Informative, vital information for all educators, counselors, health care professionals, police officers, and everyone concerned with child abuse. John Seryak wrote this book for you. Read it and learn 'the signs' that we've all seen and suspected."

Officer Ed Wilson, D.A.R.E. Officer
Bath Police Dept., Akron, Ohio

"Children cannot be expected to protect themselves from sexual abuse and molestation; adults must protect children from sexual predators.

In many instances, the sexual abuse and molestation is so misunderstood and overwhelming to young children that they are unable to put the situation into words to tell a trusted adult. Teachers have to believe that they will be the front line of support and revelation in these situations for many children. Children talk to us by actions and behaviors as well as, and even more importantly than, their words.

Teachers should not be afraid to ask a child what is going on in their lives in response to noticed and different behaviors. Teachers see hundreds of children over many years and are the best qualified individuals to know when a specific child's behavior is different and unexplained.

The sooner children and families can get help in sexual molestation situations the sooner the healing process can begin. The majority of child sexual abuse victims are not able to confront these issues and deal with them through counseling until adulthood. This is due in large part because no caring adult interceded on their behalf to address this terrifying situation.

Teachers, trust your observation skills, and what your heart tells you about a specific child. If you believe that something is the matter in a child's life, it probably is. Don't be afraid to become that one significant and caring adult that can make all the difference in that child's life.

This book should be must reading for every teacher, not just for information but as input and verification that these children do exist in every classroom in this country. Children need our help to tell their story and to get the counseling they so desperately need to begin the road to healing and wholeness.

I know, because I have been there. I too, am a survivor of childhood sexual molestation and no one interceded on my behalf; not teachers, not neighbors, not family."

Mary Ellen Atwood, Ph.D.
Professor Emeritus and Research Professor
College of Education – The University of Akron

DEAR TEACHER
If You Only Knew!

Adults Recovering From Child
Sexual Abuse Speak To Educators

Revised & Expanded

By John M. Seryak, M.Ed.

Published by
The Dear Teacher Project
PO Box 11
Bath, Oh 44210-0011

© 1999 John M. Seryak
Library of Congress 99-93533
ISBN 0-9659421-1-2

Edited by: Kristen J. Seryak
Cover Design: Jim Shoulak & John M. Seryak
Haiku by: John M. Seryak

First Printing August, 1997.
Second Printing September, 1999.

Printed in the United States of America.

Ruth,
Thanks for your
support of Dear Teacher!
JH

ACKNOWLEDGMENTS

The concept of The Dear Teacher Project was realized through the work and support of many friends and acquaintances. I would like to give special thanks to:

the courageous writers of the <u>Dear Teacher</u> letters. Their encouragement by word and deed shows a valued interest in furthering the education of teachers.

my colleagues in the field who read the material and chose to become awakened to the challenges of the presence of abused students in their classrooms.

my personal and professional counselor and mentor, Dick, for his honest and intuitive constructive comments.

my close personal friends, Mary Jane and Fred, for their encouragement and belief in this work.

my dear friend and support group co-founder Larry for his support.

my wife, Roseann, and children, Claire, Kristen, Tom, John, Mary, and Faith for their patient understanding and help along the way.

my daughter Kristen, for her dedication and enthusiasm in the editing process of this book.

my friend, running partner and business mentor, Joe, whose support was integral in the production of this book.

all the child advocates I have come to know through whose example I have taken strength and courage.

ABOUT THE AUTHOR

John Seryak has taught in the public school system for 28 years. His graduate studies were completed in Curriculum and Instruction with a concentrated study of child sexual abuse issues.

The current focus of John's research is raising teacher awareness of sexually abused students. He continues to research, write, and provide staff development for educators.

John also writes poetry relating to child sexual abuse, the recovery process, and personal/spiritual growth. His work has been published in a variety of journals and newsletters. He performs his poetry in coordination with the dance movements of his wife, Roseann.

John, Roseann and their six children live in Ohio.

TABLE OF CONTENTS

FORWARD

It was a time for decision making; to take a look at career goals and opportunities. I had taught in the nation's public school system for more than 20 years. I had the time and desire to plan for a career after my classroom teaching years. I decided that 30 years in the classroom was a complete and fulfilling "first career." Yet, at the age of 52 I would certainly be too young and healthy in mind, body, and spirit to retire full time.

Many career options were considered: counseling, law school, administration, supervision, and religious ministry. After much inner reflection, I came to accept the fact that I was, pure and simply, an educator. I chose to begin my graduate studies to receive a master's degree in education (having married as soon as I began teaching and immediately starting a family and raising six children, my time commitments and financial situation prevented me from starting my graduate studies earlier). My receiving a master's degree was never intended to create the status of additional letters after my name, nor was it a goal, primarily, to receive a higher pay scale on my continuing contract. I fully intended, from the start, to make my graduate education meaningful and productive in the education profession. My personal life situation leant its experience to guide me into a challenging direction.

For four years prior to my decision to enter graduate studies, I had been on my own "self-prescribed study" program in regard to the issues of childhood sexual abuse and neglect. My intense interest in physical, emotional, and sexual abuse came about as a result of being a supporter to my wife. She was in the process of recovering, as an adult, from childhood physical, sexual, emotional and spiritual abuses. Eventually, our entire family became involved in the recovery process: private, couples, and family counseling programs. The odyssey of our family's road to healing is continuing into the present. That is a whole story unto itself. The work of the healing process presented many new and valuable insights for me, as a professional.

As a "self-confirmed" educator, questioning my future role in the field, I came to the realization that I needed to express the knowledge I had gained. Books, workshops, conferences, professional journals, newsletters, personal contacts, public forum "speak-out" programs, and my experience of living with a "Survivor" all brought about a full and intense understanding of the nature of childhood abuses and the traumas they create. I had come to learn so much about the symptomology and long-term destructive effects from child abuse experiences. Inexorably, what came forth was the concept of reaching out to my colleagues. I wanted to share with them, to educate them, and to increase their awareness about the realities of childhood abuse and neglect in the lives of our students.

Having had many experiences in speaking with adults in recovery from such abuses, and speaking with their families and other supporters, I knew as adults, they had valuable information and knowledge to share with professionals. As a teacher, their words helped me look at my classroom of students in a healthier way. Their stories allowed me to "see" certain behaviors and reactions in my students, which I had not noticed previously. With this awareness I chose to act and react in a different way with my students. I will share this specifically in the reflection sections after the <u>Dear Teacher</u> letters.

INTRODUCTION

It is 7:25 a.m. as I stand by my classroom door watching the hundreds of students coming through the hall of my middle school. This morning I am keenly aware of the unpleasant statistics that are a reality in some of the students' lives.

This morning's newspaper featured a story I've read all too often. A young girl reports her father to the authorities for sexually abusing her. Facts sighted in the article bring statistics to life.

I watch as my students file into the room — fourteen boys and 12 girls. Which ones are abused and neglected? Rarely, if ever will any teacher know for sure.

As I take attendance, my attention is drawn to certain students. Shawna stares blankly ahead, zombie-like. Not so unusual for this early in the morning, but I recall other things about her. She has above average absence and tardiness. Her incomplete school work, crying jags, stomachaches, psychosomatic blindness, and faltered gate all add to observations that greatly concern me. She has told me something is wrong, but she doesn't know what. Even with the help of the school counselor, her mother, and a private therapist, Shawna is troubled.

Jimmy is already drawing on his arm in jet-black ink. He will later paint his lips black only to be sent to the restroom to remove the ink. He continues to verbalize the desire to set classroom pets on fire. He angrily speaks of his mother as a lesbian and a graduate from the school of "jack-off." Jimmy disrupts more classes than I can count.

Bill sits quietly and focused, but then the blaring morning announcements startle him into an outrageous outburst. His profanity doesn't fit a sixth-grade environment; neither does his behavior as he begins to run wildly around the room touching students and property. He shows no respect for either.

Suzy sits motionless. She melts into ambiguity so no one sees her. Somehow she completes her work consistently with above average grades. She rarely if ever speaks and then it is barely audible.

Betsy is bubbling over with enthusiasm. She is ever ready to begin the day. She earns straight A's in all her subjects including art, gym, and music. Her out of school social and club activities are scheduled into her very short day. "She is a pleasure to have in class," is a comment imbedded on every report card.

Are these the faces of abused and neglected children? There are certainly signs that would lead a teacher to question further—deeper. The spectrum of symptoms is long; spanning diagnosed Severe Behavior Disorder to compulsive perfectionism. There are abused and/or neglected students in every classroom in America—period.

A child is like a jigsaw puzzle. Piece after piece is spread out year after year, classroom after classroom. Most of the time a single teacher sees only a few of the multiple pieces making up a student's totality.

Any one behavior a student exhibits does not in and of itself signal a symptom of abuse. If, however, we collect many pieces from our colleagues through team meetings and conferences we may formulate an accurate picture of each student.

One in three girls will be sexually abused before the age 18. One in six or seven boys will be sexually abused in his youth.

Every year more than one million reports are made to social service agencies involving nearly 3 million children.

More than three children die each day as a result of abuse or neglect.

Of all substantiated cases of child maltreatment, 44 percent were for neglect, 24 percent for physical abuse, 15 percent for sexual abuse, and 17 percent of other forms.

Effects of child abuse are often obvious decades later in the form of mental, physical and social dysfunctions.

Teacher recognition and appropriate response to student behaviors will make a difference for those in need. It is a duty of the teaching profession to awaken to the overwhelming facts and effects of abuse and neglect.

The <u>Dear Teacher Project</u> was conceived to reach out and speak to educators in a clear and enlightening format. The idea was to collect letters to an imagined or real teacher from adults recovering from childhood sexual abuse and neglect experiences. The imagined teacher acted as a surrogate for all real teachers. Through the responses of the contributors, all teachers could benefit from the message.

The letter writers were asked to share their classroom and life experiences with teachers. Anecdotal experiences might help increase teacher awareness of important issues from abused students. I asked for reflective experiences from grade levels K-12.

Using sources collected over the years, I wrote to many support groups, recovery newsletter editors and publishers, and professional organizations. Their cooperation in "networking" about the Dear Teacher Project to recovering adults was warmly received. I began receiving phone calls and letters from all across the United States. The enlightened stories in the letters and poems about school experiences were gratifying and expected. The writers shared their stories in personal, intimate, and poignant voices. Surely, teachers like myself would "see" within these stories some of their own students past, present, and future. Soon after beginning the project, I realized that educators could formulate new and varied teaching strategies. And surely, these teachers would develop a new awareness and choose healthier ways to communicate with students. Awakening educators to the realities of the abuse in the lives of their students is one of the primary goals of Dear Teacher. With this realization, teachers will choose to act/react in a healthier manner.

The letters focus on the student experiences these survivors had in the classroom. The submitters speak clearly and concisely to teachers about what their life experience was at the time they were attending school. All letters are printed as they were received and no changes were made other than editing for typographical errors or misspellings. If any changes did occur, it was with the written permission of the submitter.

Within these pages the lives of surviving adults reveal issues of childhood abuse. It is a topic that is still kept all too secret in our society. This issue of secrecy is discussed in, Handbook of Clinical Intervention in Child Sexual Abuse, by Suzanne M. Sgroi, M.D., (1982). Being secretive about abuse is a way to minimize both for perpetrators and for educators. If we don't see it, touch it, smell it, or taste it, we don't have to respond to it. Like death and cancer, abuse is covered in the media, but is an unpleasant topic of conversation to be avoided. This is understandable. No one wants to believe that our students could be treated in abusive ways that would affect them for the rest of their lives. As educators, we are just like anyone else. We turn away from the horrors of childhood abuse.

However, the situation is this: in America, childhood traumatic abuse is at epidemic proportions. According to the Ohio Department of Health, the working definition for the term epidemic is: The occurrence of cases/incidences in numbers greater than expected in a particular population or for a particular period of time. The organization, CIVITAS, in partnership with the Baylor College of Medicine, published, "Last year (1994) in the United States more than 3 million children were reported as victims of child abuse or neglect. That's a 300 percent increase since 1982." With statistics in most studies documenting childhood abuses of most kinds to be well above expected numbers, we are faced with a very significant social ill. Ruth Herman Wells, MS in her article, "The Invisible Epidemic," *Adolescence* May, (1993), defines and discusses the insidious reality of incest in the lives of adolescents. Studies conducted by Diana E.H. Russell, The Secret Trauma, (1986) found 38 percent of women having experienced unwanted sexual experiences before age 18. The U.S. Department of Health and Human Service's publication, "The Role of Educators in the Prevention and Treatment of Child Abuse and Neglect" cites from a 1986 study that 1,424,400 children were known to have suffered maltreatment nationally. The National Clearinghouse on Child Abuse and Neglect Information states that, " Since 1980, reports of child abuse and neglect have more than doubled."

Whatever numbers, statistics, and data you are familiar with, there is one certain basic truth that stands out: Nearly all children who experience traumatic life experiences attend school. The teaching profession puts educators on the "FRONTLINES." Teachers are frequently the first responsible adults to observe and recognize the behaviors and symptoms of abuse and neglect.

For our purpose trauma is defined as the event(s) that a student experiences which cause life-long effects requiring treatment for a healing process. In our society this mostly occurs in abuse or neglect situations: physical, sexual, emotional, and spiritual.

Recently our profession has given us many "Hats" to wear. This is neither appropriate nor fitting. Teachers are NOT counselors, therapists, psychologists, doctors, social workers, or private investigators. We are teachers! Our professionalism depends on us understanding our position and keeping healthy professional boundaries.

The Dear Teacher Project fostered insights about the relationship of a classroom teacher and students living through traumatic life experiences:

1. An educator's main duty is to provide creative, challenging, and enriching classroom experiences for students.

2. Educators are in a sacred, trusted position. Students look to classroom teachers, as role models, to be rational, sane, centered adults who can be trusted and provide stability.

3. A significant percentage of students have experienced traumas that will continue to affect them for the rest of their lives.

4. As a society we do not want to believe or deal with the reality of childhood abuses (IT IS JUST TOO PAINFUL), and teachers are ill trained to recognize subtle signs of abuse.

5. Observations of the effects of sexual abuse are difficult. Additional training for teachers is necessary. Children are able to hide their trauma skillfully, often a result of shame and fear.

6. Teachers are faced with a dilemma. If on the one hand, they suspect abuse and report the incident, the response by overburdened agencies may be inadequate. The result becomes potentially greater abuse for the student or hostility towards the teacher; however, failure to report a suspicion of abuse is illegal and unethical.

7. Students may fail to identify their trauma due to: their experience is the only one they know and this appears "normal" to them; they may have traumatic amnesia or repression as a survival technique to protect their holistic psychic system.

8. Teachers need be healthy adults in body, mind, and spirit. Being alert to student behaviors and their causes can be stressful and exhausting. This could set up a teacher to react in an inappropriate or even abusive manner.

9. Teachers must act when it has become apparent that a student has experienced trauma of some sort. Teachers must have a preplanned network of resources to advise them about the proper and most suitable action to take.

10. The identification, reporting and intervention process for abused children needs to be improved. Educators, children service agencies, law enforcement, and families must coordinate and cooperate more fully with each other.

Each of the above premises is addressed in my reflections on the Dear Teacher letters. As you read through the experiences and reflections of the letters, one of the purposes of <u>Dear Teacher</u> is to clarify boundaries and job descriptions of our vocation as educators. Your own reflections, observations, and follow-up actions are of the utmost importance for the present and future of your classroom experiences. You may see evidences immediately of hidden traumas in students, or as your experience broadens you may even recognize previously unrecognized behaviors. This new awareness has an importance that may help define how to react and formulate appropriate reactions to classroom students.

The format for this work entails a brief introduction to the author of the letter. Their story is then presented in its entirety. I will comment on what I see as significant. It must be stressed that this is not a psychological analysis of the writers or their words. The letters' main purpose is to give the reader an insight to help understand the abused student's behavior.

As this is the new revised edition of *Dear Teacher, If You Only Knew!* I have reformatted the book into two parts. Part I entitled, "Professionally Speaking," contains letters from academic and medical professionals who specifically engage in child sexual abuse issues. These letters affirm and validate the need for continued awareness education in regard to child sexual abuse. Part II consists of my original book with the addition of new letters received after the 1st printing of <u>*Dear Teacher...*</u>

Part I

Professionally Speaking

Over the past year and a half, with the release of <u>Dear Teacher, If You Only Knew!</u> I have had the privilege of networking with professionals in the field of child advocacy. These professionals are from the academic as well as the medical fields. It is heartening to know that the concern for the prevention and intervention of child sexual abuse is of prime concern in these fields of practice.

In particular, Michael and Ilene Berson, and Mic Hunter, have been a great support of **The Dear Teacher Project** and its mission of creating awareness for the education community in regard to the issues of child sexual abuse. Recently Michael and Ilene were appointed to an advisory committee for the United Nations. The Child Health Task Force Advisory Committee is a component of the initiative entitled, "Innocence in Danger," an online global Internet education and safety program for children and their families.

One of the benefits the Internet provides is the communication ease of meeting colleagues in any given field. It was such my luck, or synchronized blessing, to have met Michael, Ilene, and Mic over the Internet. Through myriad contacts and connections, we were introduced as having common inspirations and goals. The professional and personal sharing we have experienced has been supportive and rewarding.

Dr. Victoria Codispotti became a contact professional and supporter of <u>Dear Teacher</u> through my counselor and mentor Rev. Richard D. Clewell, D.Min.

I appreciate and welcome the following letters from such esteemed colleagues. Their professionalism and dedication to the prevention and intervention of child sexual abuse is exemplary. I consider myself privileged to be is such company.

Michael and Ilene Berson

"Recognizing and Responding to Child Maltreatment: A Teacher's Challenge to Care."

The safety and well being of children is of paramount importance. This sentiment is often touted by education professionals as a creed of their profession; however, the reality of practice is that few professionals are prepared for their role as protectors and advocates for children. As the history below details, acknowledgement of abuse has encountered societal barriers, and continues to interfere with personal and professional standards of care in schools and communities.

A Brief History

The case of Mary Ellen Wilson is often cited as the initiation of state intervention on behalf of abused and neglected children. Mary Ellen had been physically abused by her foster parents; however, in the 1870s no state or federal legislation was enacted which addressed the needs of children who had been abused and victimized. Conversely, laws existed to protect the well being and ensure the proper care of animals. Therefore, in an attempt to create an environment of physical and emotional safety for Mary Ellen, the child was referred to the Society for the Prevention of Cruelty to Animals. Based on a court order, Mary Ellen was removed from her abusive home under the auspices that she be recognized as an animal and therefore entitled to protection under the animal cruelty legislation. As a result of the Mary Ellen case, the New York Society for the Prevention of Cruelty to Children was founded in 1874 and set the stage for the child protection movement in the United States. Although the Society for the Prevention of Cruelty to Children was formed in the late 1800s, child abuse and neglect did not begin to receive increased attention which led to child abuse legislation until the 1960s when Dr. Henry Kempe and his colleagues identified a new medical diagnosis—battered child syndrome. Battered child syndrome was associated with children who presented with injuries for which parents' explanations were insufficient or contradictory to the pattern of injury. Concurrently, reports emerged about the failure of physicians to identify and report child abuse to the appropriate authorities. This publicity captured the attention of medical professionals, the general public, and lawmakers. By 1966 all of the states in our nation but one had enacted legislation mandating physicians to report suspected child maltreatment. The first federal child abuse legislation in 1974 served as the catalyst for expanding child abuse legislation in many of the states and resulted in setting the standard for state mandatory reporting laws. Subsequently, state laws broadened the range of professionals legally obligated to make reports regarding suspected child abuse and neglect. These laws have been based on the premise that protection and services to children can only be provided when cases of maltreatment and abuse become known. They are the legal incentive for people to participate in the identification process.

State Statutes

All states share some core components in their mandatory reporting laws, including definitions of abusive situations, delineation of conditions in which reporting is required, identification of mandatory reporters, descriptions of sanctions for not reporting, and statements of immunity from civil and criminal liability for good faith reports. Nonetheless, the specifics of the abuse definitions and reporting requirements diverge in subtle ways.

Who is required to report may vary for certain professional groups. The initial state legislations focused on medical professionals as mandated reporters; however, health care workers, social service professionals, and teachers were later identified as critical participants in the process of identifying abused children. Confusion also arises over what legally delineates abuse and the circumstances under which reporting is required. State laws indicate that mandatory reporters are to act when they suspect abuse. The phrase "reason to believe" emphasizes that mandated reporters do not need to establish a degree of certainty that a child has been abused. The law requires the report of reasonable suspicions, and some states specify that mandatory reporters need only report information received while in their professional capacity. Universally persons required to report suspected abuse are provided with protection from civil and criminal liabilities associated with reporting when reports are filed in good faith and there is an absence of malicious intent. This protection exists regardless of whether the abuse is substantiated on investigation. Conversely, in most states a mandated professional who knowingly fails to report is guilty of a misdemeanor and upon conviction must be fined and/or imprisoned.

Issues Interfering with the Identification of Child Abuse.

Educators may be aware of their legal responsibility as mandated reporters, but there are many issues which interfere with identifying child abuse. Although individually we would state that we value children and believe they deserve to be protected, historically, we as a society have failed to act on this belief. Society's attitudes about abuse have influenced public perception regarding the protection of children and the pervasiveness of abusive acts perpetrated against young people. We may verbalize horror at the idea of child physical or sexual abuse, but when confronted with the reality of child maltreatment, it is more comforting to deny evidence of the abuse than to take action. Our own comfort level with issues of sex and violence may lead to avoidant responses to cope with these troubling issues and situations. Additionally, many professionals are afraid of the backlash that could result from reporting suspected child abuse. We may not want to jeopardize our relationship with the adults in the child's life, and we may choose to protect our institution rather than ensure the safety of the child. However, when we put our own needs before the needs of a child, we fail to provide protection for young people who are unable to protect themselves. If abuse goes unnoticed and unreported, it is likely that it will continue and perhaps escalate.

The plight of victimized children in the classroom has been an issue of grave concern since professionals acknowledged child maltreatment and fought to establish a protective system of care. However, even though an understanding of the field of child abuse continues to evolve, there has been a tendency by institutions of education to overlook these issues and to avoid the role of child advocate. What does the teacher really know and understand about incidents of abuse experienced by children in her classroom? Even those teachers who have received training in reporting laws and their legal responsibility to act on their suspicions of maltreatment typically report that they lack an understanding of abuse dynamics, family functioning, and child protection systems. In fact, their knowledge base may be clouded by myths about abuse that leave them helpless in the face of children who desperately need competent and caring support networks. The following true case illustrates this predicament.

She was only 8 years old. Everyone described her as a sweet girl. She did as she was told, and although she wasn't the top student in her class, her academic performance was adequate. There was nothing particularly unique about this little girl, and she was the type of third grader who blended into the group. But suddenly one day, she began to stand out to the teacher. First it was the excessive absences. The teacher didn't ask why this student who always had a perfect attendance record missed sporadically and then was out for an entire week. Poor attendance was a chronic problem at this elementary school and didn't arouse a response from otherwise overburdened teachers. When the child returned to school, the student was welcomed back and then given a folder of the work that she missed. It never was completed.

The teacher became frustrated as the homework was turned in less frequently and the student became less responsive. The girl stopped raising her hand in class and barely nodded her head when called on. After a second period of chronic absences the teacher gave the child an ultimatum. "You must have a completed homework folder on my desk or there will be consequences." As an obedient child, the girl muddled through the pages of work, and put the folder in her backpack. But once at school, her memory of the homework and the threat of punishment were replaced by other intruding thoughts. She forgot to place the folder in the teacher's inbox, and the teacher responded by keeping the child after school to copy words and their definitions out of the dictionary.

The teacher received a call from the mother who reminded the teacher that the child had been absent because of her preparation for the criminal trial against the child's stepfather who had been sexually molesting her for the prior three year period. The trial had ended in a conviction of the stepfather and a 10-year sentence. The teacher acknowledged that she was aware of this situation, and she informed the mother that the child had been slacking in her schoolwork. The teacher further stated that since an excessive period of time had passed since the child had last turned in a completed assignment the child would be subjected to the usual classroom policies for discipline.

Educators may have a real fear of the cost of caring. They may want to avoid the fear, pain, and suffering that is associated with trauma experiences. The teacher is part of the child's interpersonal network which creates a powerful context for the recovery. The child's traumatic experience may be so distressing to the educator that they actually may discourage the child from discussing their abuse. When the child simultaneously lacks family support networks the outcome can be devastating. By avoiding the pain of abuse, educators, like the teacher in the case above, may prefer to focus on an area in which they feel they have control, academics.

All individuals have a need to make sense of their experience by developing comprehensible, meaningful and orderly explanations for phenomena. There is a fear among adults that they will become preoccupied with issues of cruelty and perpetration of violence on defenseless children. We are overloaded with images in the newspaper, but individuals still may be desensitized by relief that it's not someone they know. What happens when it is someone you know? A struggle to make sense out of experiences that are incomprehensible can create tremendous conflict. Disruptions in our sense of safety shatter our sacred illusion of invulnerability. Teachers who themselves have children may begin to fear for their safety and may be wary of others who come in contact with their family. Cynical beliefs may be part of the thinking of the professional. They may lose trust in basic decency, feel powerless, and helpless. They may feel rage toward the offender and feel despair about their inability to prevent abuse. The teacher in the case study may appear controlling and overly rigid in her interaction with the child due to her need to exert more influence over the student to restore her own sense of power and overcome feelings of vulnerability. If the teacher should acknowledge her struggle with abuse issues, she may find that she is isolated and alienated from other professionals who may have a sense of disdain or disbelief in maltreatment.

It is essential that educators have open forums for discussing the painful issue associated with child maltreatment. The difficulty is identifying colleagues who can similarly acknowledge these feelings and discuss how work of this nature affects them personally and professionally.

Conclusion

Child abuse laws exist to provide protection for children who cannot protect themselves. This legislation provides an opportunity and gives permission to professionals to act on the belief that children are valued and deserve to be protected. If a child is a victim of abuse, the filing of a report is a critical means to access help for the child and family.

Educators serve as the first line of defense in the identification and reporting of child maltreatment. As mandated reporters educators are legally required to protect children by reporting suspicions of abuse, but reporting abuse is only one aspect of the necessary multidisciplinary, community-wide effort to address the serious problem of child victimization. By acquiring additional knowledge of their responsibilities and the implications of maltreatment on their students in the middle school setting, teachers can play an important role in stemming the tide of abuse.

Recognizing the tremendous needs of children for supportive services, we as practicing professional have a special obligation to our students and trainees to prepare them for the realities of child maltreatment. Through this process we may begin the difficult task of transforming traumatized children from states of sadness, depression, and desperation to hope, joy, and a renewed sense of purpose and meaning of life.

Michael J. Berson, Ph.D. is an Assistant Professor of Social Science Education in the Department of Secondary Education at the University of South Florida. Michael's publications and research interests include technology in social studies education, the use of primary source materials in instruction, and global child advocacy. He has collaborated on the development of a training model to prepare educators to support children who have been victimized.

Ilene R. Berson, Ph.D. is on the faculty of the Department of Child and Family Studies at the Louis de la Parte Florida Mental Health Institute at the University of South Florida. She is Director of the Florida child protection team sexual abuse curriculum project and collaborates on the development of training for nonmental health professionals. Her research focuses on the decision making process of educators as mandated reporters and creating safe, supportive school environments for child victims.

Mic Hunter

Dear Teacher,

I am extremely glad that you are reading this book. Merely by reading one book you are gaining more information on childhood sexual abuse than most psychiatrists, social workers, psychologists, and marriage and family therapists receive during their entire graduate training. Although I have four degrees, and hold three treatment provider licenses, I have never been required to obtain any education on the topic of child sexual abuse!

We used to believe that childhood sexual abuse was rare. Unfortunately, we were mistaken. It has been only recently that researchers have documented that the sexual abuse of children is all too common in American society. We used to believe that the perpetrator of sexual abuse was the 'dirty old man' lurking around the playground leering at little girls. We now know that the majority of sexual abuse is perpetrated by an adult known to the child, that both boys and girls are victimized, and that women as well as men commit sex crimes against children. We used to believe that incest only happened in poorly educated isolated backwoods families. We were shocked to find that children from all ethnic, geographic, financial, and social groups are at risk for being sexually abused in their own homes.

Imagine a woman who is raped and then each year sends the man who sexually assaulted her a birthday card. Most of us would be disturbed by this and think, "What a bizarre act!" But that is exactly what the girl who has been incested does. She gives her rapist a birthday card, a father's day card, and has breakfast with him. This too is a disturbing act, yet it happens in my community, and in your community as well.

This school year you have students who were, or are being sexually abused. You were among victims of sexual abuse the first day you were a student teacher, you will be with sexual abuse victims on the very last day before you retire. To realize that some of the children under your care have experienced sexual abuse is unsettling. Most teachers become career educators because they like children, and want to help them. The idea that someone, perhaps even a family member, is abusing a child is repugnant to most teachers. I know this because every year I read numerous papers written by teachers seeking a masters degree in education, who tell me, "I had no idea sexual abuse was so common. Now that I know the signs and symptoms I think of all the students I have taught who may have been abused. There are so many possible victims I overlooked. I wish I had known what to do back then!"

The idea that is most shocking to the teachers who attend my course on childhood sexual abuse is that some of their fellow educators are sexually abusing students. "Is there no safe place? Not the home, not the school?" they exclaim. Unethical teachers can only continue to abuse children in schools where the other teachers turn a blind eye to the signs that student abuse may be taking place. When you see a teacher who spends excessive time with one particular student, is constantly touching students, making sexual comments about students' bodies, or trying to be more a buddy to students rather than being an adult role model, talk to the teacher. You may prevent that teacher from going further and becoming sexual with a student. If the behavior continues let your principal know what you have observed.

The task of identifying and assisting those students who have been sexually abused must seem like an overwhelming requirement. As a teacher you are already expected to do a great deal for your students. You are given many responsibilities, yet few resources. But let me reassure you. The best thing you can do to help the victim of childhood abuse is to do what you are doing right now, getting information on what constitutes abuse, the symptoms commonly are shown by those who have been victimized, and how to report suspected abuse to the proper authorities. Do for the child what the child can not do for her or himself.

Remember as a teacher you may actually spend more time in the presence of these children than do their parents. You act as role model for your students. You may be the only adult in their lives who treats them with respect, who does not engage in intrusive touch, yelling, or name calling. Just providing an example of a safe adult can be a life-saver for an abused child.

Mic Hunter, Psy.D. is Adjunct Program Professor at Saint Mary's University in Minneapolis. He is a licensed psychologist, marriage and family therapist, and an alcohol and drug counselor. He is author of **Abused Boys: The Neglected Victims of Sexual Abuse,** and editor of The Sexually Abused Male, Volume I & II, Adult Survivors of Sexual Abuse: Treatment Innovations, and Child Survivors and Perpetrators of Sexual Abuse.

Victoria Codispotti

Sometimes it is impossible to believe that someone could harm the children we so lovingly care for. And to think that someone would sexually abuse our children is even more obscene. Yet these men (and women) who hurt our children often sit beside us, live among us, and love our children as well as their own. But they also hurt them, damage them psychologically, and betray precious trusts. We often see no signs from the offenders themselves. But we **do** see the signs and the symptoms in our children.

Children in our schools are being harassed, molested, and abused. Some by their own family members, grandparents, their church leaders, their teachers, their brothers and sisters. It is imperative that we become aware and recognize the signs of abuse in children. We can no longer afford to deny our intuitions, or ignore the subtle comments of our children, who no longer wish to spend time with an adult who was once a "friend."

Teachers and counselors understand that child abuse is on the rise! Offenders are bright, manipulative, and prey on those most precious to us. They "hang out" where our children play - malls, restrooms, video stores, game stores, baseball parks, and skating rinks. They feign friendliness, they befriend the child who is most alone, or sits away from the crowd. And the offender who is a family member confuses the child, befriends him/her, and teachers the child it is dangerous to speak about this atrocity. Our children are coerced; they are laden with fear. Who would believe them? Who would help them? Who will recognize their unhappiness, their fear, their difficulties with attention, their sensitivity to touch or caring remarks?

It is imperative that we **PAY ATTENTION** to our children. Do not be afraid to ask questions, to give them a safe place to talk and ask questions. Adulthood is too long to wait for the resolutions of the pain that robs them of their self-esteem and their ability to have relationships. Adulthood is too long to wait for healing.

Victoria Codispotti, M.D., F.A.P.A.,CCHP has a private practice and specializes in psychosexual behavior. She is also assistant professor at NEOUCOM (North East Ohio University College of Medicine.)

NAKED TRUTH

Souls bared and naked

Survivors now – victims then

Teachers, please listen.

Part II

Dear Teacher, If You Only Knew!

Chapter I
ANNE

My first response to the <u>Dear Teacher Project</u> came as a phone call from Anne M. Cox. She called from California one Saturday afternoon introducing herself as a private publisher and political activist for the issue of childhood abuse. She was very encouraging about the possibilities of the <u>Dear Teacher</u> <u>Project</u>. With great poise, she proceeded to read the letter she wrote. I listened intently and marveled at the content and teaching messages it contained. Every letter and interview since then has increased my awareness of the challenges students face in the light of living with abuse and neglect.

Anne's letter contains issues of trust, fear, dysfunction, hidden physical pain, outward emotional pain, and hope-filled recovery. I invite you to read Anne's letter.

Dear Teacher,

You may not know this about me: I went through 11 years of school having to rely on my fingers to add and subtract. Forget division and multiplication. I couldn't solve such problems. (And, to date, I don't know how to calculate for leaving a tip at a restaurant.) I wasn't lacking comprehension skills or intelligence. It was that my parents kept me home from school so frequently that I couldn't keep up with my classmates; it was that I feared telling anyone that I couldn't see what was written in chalk on the blackboard when my desk was at the back of the classroom; it was that I didn't know how to relate to children my age to ask for their help with homework or classroom assignments because my parents moved our family nearly every other year, and I didn't know how to make friends; it was that there were plenty of addition and subtraction problems presented on tests that helped me earn marginal, passing grades.

I was the child who missed, not skipped, kindergarten, since my parents refused to meet the school district's requirement that I wear protective headgear because of a flaw in the formation of my skull, a medical condition. I was the little girl who went to first-grade and was too frightened to raise my hand to ask if I could go to the bathroom and I wet myself instead. (My parents' displays of verbal and physical battering had instilled in me that it was best to not ask for anything, and I didn't dare make a move without their permission; I learned how to behave properly in public places. A store was my first classroom; my father beat me, as other adults passed down the same aisle nonchalantly, if I moved from the spot in which he told me to stand. My parents were omniscient, I believed.) I was the one who could not—and still cannot—remember the first-grade teacher's name; there were three or four. I'm sorry, I didn't keep very good score.

I was the third-grade student who excelled in reading and writing until the teacher accused me of cheating; the fourth-grader who refused to read anymore and who clung to the teacher by the end of the year because only she didn't laugh when I mispronounced certain words and I couldn't explain the theme or plot of the books I pretended to have read, which she seemed to sense. I was the child in fifth grade who sat on the sidelines at recess, who appeared tired, who told my teacher that my father was dead (though he wasn't) because I didn't want to get in trouble for not going to school when my parents made me stay home because I was sore or bleeding too much. I was the same little girl who was reprimanded following "show-and-tell" because I admitted one day, "My father makes me eat rotten meat," and no one believed me after he was called to the school and said, "She's lying."

Yes, it was me, the child who was caught more than once returning to school late after lunch because I went to a convenience store down the street to steal food; I also broke into someone's home and invaded the refrigerator. I didn't think I could tell anyone why I was late and I was punished (given more homework than I could possibly finish since I had to take care of my mother and father at night). And there I was, in fifth and sixth grades, towering above all my classmates who may have believed that calling me "Olive Oil" and "toothpick" were terms of endearment. The only thing I was, was hungry, yet no one could see it.

By sixth grade, I spent more time in the principal's office than in the classroom it seemed. The essays I wrote were all wrong. The principal asked: "Where did you learn that?!?" "Who told you that?!?" "Where did you see that?!?" I was a child of the 1960s, with conservative (authoritarian) parents. The school viewed their word as gospel and accepted their explanation for one of my "imaginative" essays, for example, titled, "Behind the Green Door," all about the activities of the nude people roaming around in my "active imagination." The principal was very impressed: He held a number of conferences—with teachers, secretaries, my parents and their "li'l storyteller." I was rewarded, assigned to classes for "gifted" students.

I was sent home from school with a note for my mother from my PE teacher the last day of the first week of seventh grade. It said that I would fail gym class if I didn't wear the proper clothing, the suggestion was that my mother buy me a bra. I returned instead with a note that excused me from participating in physical education activities. And, once again, we moved.

At my new school, I wrote more. Starvation, fires, orphaned children: Those were some of the topics I picked to address in seventh and eighth grades. Writing went well, but math and science, pure hell (and I took physics in college and passed easily). I doubt that I was "lazy" or "dumb" as some students and teachers teased. I think my brain was exhausted. I couldn't think during the day; the middle-of-the-night rages and rapes kept me up too late. School was a break from the horrors at home, where sleeping simply wasn't the safe or the sane thing to do. Yet, no one at school knew by the darkness encircling my eyes and my ashen skin tone.

All the times I was late for classes during high school, well, I missed the bus and had to walk. I didn't tell anyone that I had asked my mother to drive me, only she screamed, "Don't bug me! Go away! Leave me alone!" I wasn't assertive; I was extremely scared. I didn't know that I could've gone into the administration building and explained: "My mother was sleeping when I asked her for a ride since I missed the bus. She doesn't want me around. She sleeps with a pair of real long, shiny, silver scissors under her pillow and I'm afraid to ask if she'll change her mind about driving me to school." My choice was to walk rather than to ask her again and risk angering her more.

The number of in-class assignments that I didn't complete, I can't even begin to count. I thought the reason that I couldn't grasp a pencil or pen very well was because my fingers were still numb from the chill and moisture in the air. But, once my hands warmed up, I believed that I would catch up. My ability to perform suffered, and my lousy grades plummeted even farther. I hadn't considered that my fingers may have been hurt as I attempted blocking my father's—inches wide—leather belt with my hands as he hit me. I didn't know then that children and adolescents could be affected by arthritis (which may manifest from repeated stress or injury to the body), and that my inability to sit comfortably for stretches of time could be a medical condition (arthritis affecting my hands, hips and sternum diagnosed—by a rheumatologist—as a young adult).

I don't know how I could've been missed. I didn't blend with the crowd. Most of the time I stood out; I was alone, surrounded by flocks of students and teachers, during school hours. That I ever made friends was a miracle, though most friendships were rather short-lived. One year, I'd be at one school, and then, before I knew it, we were moving—in the middle of the year, sometimes in the middle of the night. My father was not in an occupation that required relocating and uprooting continuously; he's worked for the same company (at the same site) from the 1960s to the present. No one noticed all the abrupt moves reflected in the school transcripts transferred from one district to another and another and on and on. No one questioned it, though there was a pattern that had emerged; my parents continued moving from the time I was a toddler till I ran away from home at age 16 (which is when they stopped relocating themselves).

While it's understandable how subtle indicators or potential signs of abuse and child maltreatment could go unnoticed by school personnel, it's more difficult for me to accept how obvious or blatant trauma to a child might be overlooked.

Throughout high school, writing remained my primary medium for trying to release pain, my utmost effort to "tell" what was happening to me at home. I was kept after school one day, in tenth-grade, at the request of my teacher. She wanted to discuss with me a paper I'd written about an abortion. We talked about it in-depth. I'd also spoken with the high school principal. He had become a confidant. Once a week, he and the vice-principal even attended my gourmet foods cooking class to test what I'd made. I thought nothing bad could happen with them around. As long as they were present on campus, my world felt more secure.

The feeling was shattered when one of my teachers stood in front of two classes—in which I was enrolled—and repeated things to all the students about my life at home that I'd told the principal in confidence. I didn't know the words betrayed or violation applied to the situation until I became an adult, but it was the most excruciating emotional pain I'd felt from a source outside my family. Boys in the classes started rumors about me, which inspired many students and teachers to "believe" that I was "easy" or promiscuous. I hated having to go to my classes with the teacher making slimy comments about me in front of everyone. I started to walk out after one of his stand-up routines. He stopped me and said, "You don't have a hall pass." I left anyway, and he reported me to the dean. I failed his classes and was referred to remedial classes and, as a result, withstood the beatings and sexual assaults from my father.

I devoted the eleventh grade to getting drunk, which I didn't attempt to mask from anyone at school or at home. I had alcohol on campus and drank it there; I placed the empty bottles on top in the garbage cans. I didn't try hiding anything. I didn't care anymore. I'd been suspended twice and nearly expelled.

I ran away from home (as I had done when I was 8 years old). The principal knew the reason; I sat in his office and we talked about it. He gave me the telephone number for the private line directly to his office. Oh, it wasn't that he wanted to help me. He offered me the number in case I changed my mind and wanted to engage in sexual activity with him. My mistake was in telling him that I was living with a man—I was led to believe was in his 40s but was actually in his 50s. The point is: I was a minor. The principal was aware of the abuse I experienced at home and of the living arrangements I'd made since running away from home, and since my parents refused to have me living with the them unless I met their list of 25 conditions they enumerated on paper. A law was in effect (I've discovered as an adult) that mandated that school personnel report suspected cases of child abuse to authorities. The principal didn't. Nor did the teacher with whom I'd spoken of the abortion. Two educators were aware of the subtle and obvious signs of abuse, yet didn't act responsibly on the information.

A teacher I'd had, at a different high school, lived in the same area as me. I went to his house after I'd run away from home. I didn't speak with him about the abuse. Yet, when I saw him again after I'd been living with a man roughly 30 years my senior, he had information available that clearly indicated abuse was ever-so-present. He knew that I was still a minor, and he was the next door neighbor of the man's sister; he knew how much older the man was. No report was made. (I left the man with whom I'd been living. He was subsequently arrested and pleaded no contest/nola contendre to charges of child molestation in a case involving a 10-year-old girl; he's now a registered sex offender.)

I'm not certain the nature of trauma a child experiences is "hidden." I think, more often, it's overlooked. Getting involved is a challenge—emotionally.

As I reflect and think of the teachers who may have realized something wasn't quite right or that abuse may have been occurring, I wish that they would have acted on what they might have suspected or even knew. At the same time, however, I understand why they wouldn't want to get involved. Child maltreatment is potentially volatile; it's domestic violence. Abusive or neglectful parents may regard their children as property and emotions are inflamed by parents not wanting others to interfere in the control of their "property." My parents were violent, not only toward me, but also overtly abusive toward their siblings and acquaintances, to whom their abuse of me was patently clear.

Educators who filled a role in my life did no less than my own adult relatives: They stayed out of "it." Getting involved might have been a dangerous proposition back then. The safeguards and protections for educators reporting reasonably suspected cases of child abuse weren't well established or as firmly in place as they are now.

Had it not been for the time I spent at school, away from home, I don't know that I would have had anywhere safe to go—to escape the emotional, physical, and sexual violence plaguing my childhood and adolescence.

Gestures that some teachers make and may consider routine might be the rays of hope a traumatized child sees shining through the bleakness. I can't multiply or divide without a calculator, but more important, I know how to add and subtract because of a first-grade teacher who gave me little plastic cars to count as I stood with my classmates who knew the answers off the tops of their heads. A teacher offered me tools that indicated giving up was not the solution. Making adjustments and discovering the choices available was the lesson I was guided toward understanding.

Teachers may be lifelines for children in crisis. Adult relatives briefly entered my life and turned away as rapidly as possible. All that I had left was school, my saving grace: I want you to know about me, the traumatized child who, somehow, survived.

ANNE

Anne's letter illustrates a tragic home environment; her parents moved often to different school districts. [She points out that her father was employed by the same company in the same location for her entire school experience. Therefore, only her school districts changed, not her geographical location.] Her frequent moves pose problems for Anne as a student. Transient students are commonplace in today's mobile society. Teachers are accustomed to making adjustments for new students. This challenge is met successfully. While on the surface, Anne's transition appears smooth; a closer look could give the teacher a clue to unusual behaviors or poor academic performance.

This obviously is only one indication of Anne's troubled family. The dysfunction and abuse went much deeper than most educators would or could have noticed.

Due to the fear Anne experienced, she wet herself in first grade. This is not uncommon for a first-grade teacher to observe, but one that a teacher may mentally store for future reference. Being aware, being observant, collecting many puzzle pieces in a child's behavior may reveal to the teacher important information for future effective intervention.

Early on, her teachers discounted Anne's call for help. This is significant. Even if teachers hear information from their students that seems implausible or unbelievable, the student is trying to tell us something. Are we listening, or do we simply dismiss it by rationalizing that the student is strange? Do we have a professional duty to document these events just in case?

Like other letters from survivors, Anne told her teachers and principal through her writing that something was not right. The school accepted the parents' explanations rather than see what might have been a possibility—subtle hints to the teacher about an unhealthy homelife. Do we read students' writing closely enough, or do we just evaluate for grammar and mechanics? What about the writers' voice and tone? Do we see? Do we hear?

Today, many schools have implemented alternative forms of evaluation. One is the portfolio. This is an excellent means of reading a student's writing history. It would aid the teacher in putting together the puzzle pieces of a student's life.

In Anne's middle school years, she is unsuccessful in math and science. Her explanation, as an adult, is that she was just too mentally exhausted. This exhaustion is mentioned frequently by other survivors in interviews. Surviving sexual, physical and psychological abuse at home requires a disproportionate amount of energy that leaves little emotional or mental power to use for academic study.

Anne did find school a "safe" and "sane" place to rest. This is so important for educators to realize. Teachers are seen by our students as safe adults to be around. Schools are a haven of safety for students. This is a very high compliment, and speaks to the sacred trust of our profession. We should accept it and own it.

Anne's tardiness is another clue among many that her family is dysfunctional and damaging. Some things in her family unit are not working properly. Missed assignments add another piece to the puzzle of Anne's life.

She wonders, " I don't know how I could've been missed." If she was noticed, no one addressed what he or she saw.

As Anne documents how her situation deteriorated, the clues or pieces to her life become even more apparent. Now, more than before, teachers must have known something was wrong; some intervention was necessary. The system failed her. What could have been done?

While not a typical scenario, the dramatic betrayal Anne experienced from one principal and the turning of other teachers' heads had to make her journey into adulthood even more difficult. The support she needed from adults in trusted positions was not available.

It is a tribute to Anne's strength as a survivor that she concludes her letter in a most positive tone with encouragement for educators. She shares with us, "Gestures that some teachers make and may consider routine might be the 'Rays of Hope' (editor's capitalization) a traumatized child sees shining through the blackness." Her negative school experiences are overshadowed by the hopeful reality that schools are safe places and teachers "may be lifelines." ·

Chapter II
ELIZABETH

Elizabeth is a 40-year-old survivor who experienced abuse and neglect from the ages of 5 to 17 while a student in Pennsylvania. She has been in the recovery process for six years. She continues communicating with me via letter. She writes, "I would like to thank you for your personal reply to my submission. I felt very honored to have had an impact on you. I feel that perhaps by sharing some of my feelings it might help just one child get what they need. If I could accomplish that, I would feel a <u>victory</u> from my suffering. I am excited by your attempt to educate the very people who have so much contact with children and who can make <u>such</u> a BIG impact on them in a <u>positive</u> way."

Elizabeth now resides in Indiana.

Dear Teacher,

I write this letter to you now as an adult, and no longer a student of yours. I also write to you as a recovered abuse survivor. While many victims may remain victims, I have aimed to put the emphasis on the term survivor. I choose to be in control of my life now. I share this with you now so that maybe you can be aware of what I went through when I was your student. I also hope that by sharing some of the feelings with you, it will give you a better understanding of what my behavior meant.

I picked you out as someone I thought of as being everything I wanted to be. I saw you as this mentor or role model. I put you up on this mentally imaged pedestal, and could see you only as ideal and perfect. I then set out to win your attention and maternal love, and to try to be just like you. I tried to reach for your attention by writing you all those little notes about a zillion little and big things. I also complimented you in grandiose proportions. I tried so hard to get you to notice me and see that I was needy and hurting. I had neither the courage nor the knowledge of how to ask you directly.

What I can remember of my feelings at the time feels so

bleak. I felt so pressured and alone when I started high school. I felt like I had to perform so highly academically since I was at Girl's High. I felt constantly reminded by my family that I was so lucky just to be there. Inside I was spiritually and emotionally devastated. I felt dead inside a lot of the time. I had no good friends when I switched to a new and bigger school. My parents were having marital problems at the time, which just piled on more anxiety and fear. To me, my mother felt like this horrible monster. I hated her so much. It felt like not one positive comment ever exited her lips. I tried so hard to be perfect to her. I cooked meals after school, baked, and kept my room immaculate. I tried to do well in school too. No matter how hard I tried, I just wasn't perfect enough or pretty enough, or my music was too corny. My hair was never just right, and it felt like I was an inferior child. So, I felt I needed to reach out to someone who would accept me without all those conditions, and that someone was you. I wanted an oasis in the middle of the nightmares, only they weren't nightmares-it was my daily life.

I didn't realize that my parents were both alcoholics. I thought all parents drank that much. I also didn't realize that not all parents yelled and hit and screamed at their kids. I also didn't realize that it wasn't my fault. I was made to think it was my fault that my mom blew up at me, and threatened me with a knife. I thought that my life was normal. My parents also made me feel that they knew everything, and were always right. I had no value within that house for my own opinion. I even believed that it was my fault that my brother was sexually abusing me. So when I got into high school, and encountered you, I realized you were different. I wasn't getting yelled at by you like my parents and previous teachers had, so I latched onto someone who felt very safe.

I sent you as clear a message as I knew how with my behavior. I needed some glimmer of sanity and caring, and what little response you gave was enough for someone starving for attention. I can't remember all the notes nor your responses, but one in particular sticks in my memory. You wrote me back a note telling me what a sweet person I was. That felt like such an enormous compliment. I took that and kept asking for more. It was enough to get me through those 4 years, and to move on in life.

So, I hope that you can see that as an abused child, I was trying to tell you something was wrong in my life. I hope it will help clue you in to help other kids you might yet encounter. I do not feel that you had the slightest clue of what I was going through, but I hope this letter will enlighten you. I feel sad and angry that you didn't have the knowledge or possibly the interest to look more closely at what was going on. I wish you had tried harder for my sake. I am lucky that you did not take advantage of me and also abuse me in any way, so for that I thank you.

I have survived my past and am intent on living my life now, not just surviving it. I feel that I have discovered how to have happiness and love in my life, and in ways that are functional and healthy. I hope that this letter gives you some idea as to what our relationship meant to me. I also hope it will educate you and that you can clearly hear my message now.

One of my conclusions from the Dear Teacher Project is addressed clearly in Elizabeth's letter. Teachers should be caring, safe, sane role models for students.

Like most students, Elizabeth couldn't ask her teachers directly for what she needed; however, she spoke to her teacher through compliments and notes.

Elizabeth's description that, " I felt dead a lot of the time," is a common statement from many survivors (Shengold, 1989). Abused and neglected children do not grow or develop in a healthy psychological and emotional way (B.D. Perry et al, 1995).

In Elizabeth's experience, school and teachers were an, "... oasis in the middle of nightmares."

Elizabeth tells us what a significant action like a teacher's complimentary note can do for a student living through home abuse and neglect. This one note from a teacher helped get her through 4 years and onto life. What dividends for a simple act that took a few minutes!

Elizabeth dichotomizes her conclusion with sadness and anger yet with grateful appreciation. She felt her teachers didn't have a clue as to her situation, but she is grateful they did not abuse her.

It is sad that her abuse was overlooked, yet equally tragic that she thanks her teachers for not abusing her. Should any student ever have to be concerned about teachers abusing? Unfortunately, yes. (A few letters address the horrific reality of teacher/student molestation and abuse.)

However, Elizabeth's new health and success in life leaves us with hope for adult survivors.

Chapter III
MIKE

Mike is a 34-year-old free-lance writer and consultant to non-profit groups in Ohio. He has been a college instructor and director of a social service agency. He states that presently he is reasonably healthy for the first time in his life, yet continues his healing process.

Dear Teacher,

First there came sexual abuse at age 8, which didn't register in me until I reached my teens. My body grew into its capacities for reproduction, stirring an awareness in me of my body as a sexual instrument. But sex now was interwoven with abuse, pain, and a subtle violence. My response was to hide and ignore my body. As I try to imagine now what symptoms the teachers in my classrooms might have noted as signs of trouble, those would be my skittishness toward physical education (the body having already betrayed me once, having already acted as a source of humiliation and shame, and the classes often structured then to mock those kids uncomfortable within their bodies), my chronic absences (not from sickness, although I tried hard to cultivate a cold or a runny nose so that I continually appeared "sickly" and so it was easier to be sent home or remain home for an extended period of time once I'd gotten my mother to make the first day's call excusing me from school), and my lack of friends.

The concern for me now in looking back on the worst of my school years (grades 6-8, no question) was that the teachers often seemed to share the popular perception of my classmates. In other words, the popular boys and girls in the eyes of the students were often absorbed as popular with the teachers as well. By the same token, the sickly and outcast remained that for the teachers as well. I didn't talk to anyone about any of my interior tumult because I wasn't convinced that I could trust the teachers, who, after all, had their hands full with discipline, with grading papers, with preparing for classes, and with releasing stress of their own.

The closest to an intervention I received came in a mastery of language. A teacher in seventh grade paid me individual attention for my creative work. This, being the first morsel of positive attention thrown to me at home or school or anywhere else, at least gave me one new and productive outlet. Instead of grinding away in misery at home with my face in a pillow, fully clothed 24 hours a day, alone and with the rooms dark, I could turn on a light and put words to paper. Not good words by my definition today, but ones that at least affirmed that I might have one capability that didn't bring me to further shame.

The gift of writing has stayed with me. It helped me through all the difficult periods of my life by allowing me an impartial space in which to place my thoughts, feelings and ideas. No one would judge these words but me, at my convenience, at my own leisure. It was the gift of a secret and intimate friend.

I wish my teachers had known more about abuse and neglect in the 1970s than they know now. I'm not sure I would have been able to recognize what was going on at home because I was still living it, defending it and thus myself. But there may have been the space created to do what I'm doing now: putting my words out into safe space where someone else might read them without the biases accorded to my body and personality, and discover whatever merit, whatever truth, lay within.

Mike.

Mike points out some behaviors that teachers may observe. Lack of friends, chronic absences, and avoidance of physical education are all common experiences noticed in any grade level. In Mike's situation, these were integrally woven from his abusive experiences.

When teachers notice these "common" clues or hints we usually don't contemplate anything beyond some difficulties in a student's social life. Maybe we need to pay closer attention. We could collect more pieces about a student's situation.

Mike notes that his teachers actually fell in line with the other students' perceptions. Because of the way Mike "felt" his teachers were reacting to him; he decided he could not trust them. Teachers saw him as others did, and they were "too busy." Are we busy? Without a doubt. Are we overloaded, overworked? At times—yes. But are teachers "too busy" for a student in need? Absolutely not! Teachers need to demonstrate to all students that if they are in need of speaking with a trusted adult, arrangements will be made.

Mike writes that creative expressions brought something positive and powerful into his life. This is common in the <u>Dear</u> <u>Teacher</u> letters. Creative expression in the classroom is vital for many abused and neglected students. (It should be noted that some students fear creative expression because they think it might let someone "see" what is happening to them. The "secret" would be revealed.)

Writing provided a format for Mike to find an impartial "safe" place. Writing one's thoughts and feelings without judgment is invaluable. Providing many opportunities for creative expressions as writing, poetry, and drawing, are valuable for all our students.

Mike isn't sure he even fully realized his own situation. Living in abuse and neglect can seem "normal" if one has no other frame of reference. The importance of a teacher's example is so crucial. To model healthy adult behaviors gives abused and neglected students another frame of reference. This reference will help them make adjustments as adults.

Mike ends his letter in a hopeful, positive tone. Recovering adults gain an uncanny wisdom to create hope for a healthy life. This has been repeatedly stated in letters to <u>Dear Teacher</u>.

Chapter IV
SAMANTHA

Samantha Ward works as a medical records technician and is a writer, poet, and model living in Alaska. Samantha suffered extreme sexual and emotional abuse from 7 to 15 years of age. She is 30 years old now and has been in recovery for more than four years.

Samantha writes, "My middle school counselor and I do write on occasion. She was the only one who listened to me from the young age of 11, and was realistic. There was nothing she could do. She wanted me to change, and do the only right things when I was ready, and take control of my life, and not to be a victim. Perhaps it was her words that finally helped me take action. I thanked her. I just wrote to her today, asking her if she still wanted to go out to lunch. She considers me a 'success story' even if I don't. It means so much to me that she thinks that about me. I want to live up to it. I am still very much a little girl. I am scared, and don't know what to say or do, sometimes because I suffered so much pain, but my Higher Power will reveal the right thing to do."

Samantha clearly brings out the valuable resource of school counselors for students. More and more we are seeing school systems providing counselors to lower grade levels.

Note the sad but real conclusion from Samantha that there was nothing the school counselor could do. Is this still true today? With increased knowledge and professional development in the childcare professions, more appropriate actions can be developed; however, there is a real sense of wisdom for the young Samantha, "...at the right time."

Samantha's fluctuating self-image is common among adults recovering from childhood abuse and neglect. It is a continuous struggle for survivors to become whole, integrated individuals. Integration is discussed in many recovery books one of which is, The Courage To Heal, (1988), by Ellen Bass and Laura Davis.

The creative writing process has been helpful to surviving victims at any age. Samantha says that her writing has been a healing outlet. She considers her poem, "Sparkling," to be one of her most beautiful expressions.

SAMANTHA

Sparkling
for my sister

My sister and I form
a secret society of pain,
linked by memories of torture
we were forced to endure
and a lack of loving
an empty feeling
That follows us wherever we go.
The secret friendships seemed like hatred
Those many years ago.
She is my perfect twin.
Our voices touch, overlap,
Sound the same, and yet again,
we are reminded of all the evil of the past
Immediately, like time transfer.
It is hard to take. We don't want to go there
Ever not in a million zillion years—it hurts.
Little blonde, green-eyed girls,
Alone, shaken, scared,
Who did not know enough to learn and understand.
It is only as women do we trust as much as we can
that nothing could separate us.
And we learn to touch base—and ask for help.
Only as grownups can we see
The horrid inhumanity
We lived through and survived.
Now I call her for voice of reason
When all along she was with me.
Seeing through her eyes—
Same twisted vision
of self and others —
That no one cared —that we were stupid,
Worthless, and not worth anyone's time.
That our bodies belong to men friends
of our mother and were not sacred to God.

DEAR TEACHER

Now a voice of reason belongs to us both,
Not crushed innocence
like broken glass,
We give back the past to ourselves as we wished it.
We recognize what we should have had.
We hold our little girls safely
in our hearts and minds.
We lay as sheets of glass
on a sunny day,
Reflecting perfectly
Sparkling openly
In the sun.

Chapter V
CLARRESSA

Another poem comes from Clarressa Beckhon Thompson, a 32-year-old-Ohioan. She is a published poet who travels and speaks on abuse issues. She is raising a wonderful family as a result of her dedicated work in the recovery process. Clarressa experienced abuse from the ages of 4-16.

Clarressa's poem, "Teacher Productivity," challenges each of us to question the integrity of teacher commitment. Often, our perception of student background is so inadequate. She enlightens us a bit more hoping we will have a better understanding of student performance.

TEACHER PRODUCTIVITY
a cry for help

TEACHER, WHY ARE YOU HERE
BECAUSE YOUR MOTHER TOLD YOU TO,
OR BECAUSE YOU THOUGHT IT PAID WELL
AND WAS SOMETHING PRODUCTIVE TO DO.

TEACHER, WHAT ARE YOU TEACHING
I REALLY CAN'T COMPREHEND,
I CAN FIND BETTER THINGS TO DO
WITH THE TIME I HAVE TO SPEND.

YOU'RE LIKE A BROKEN RECORD
REPEATING THE SAME OLD LINES,
NOT REALIZING HOW MANY OTHER THINGS
ARE TROUBLING MY MIND.

DEAR TEACHER

HOW CAN I THINK ABOUT MATH
WITH THE CONDITIONS OVER WHERE I LIVE
AND HOW CAN I THINK ABOUT SCIENCE PROJECTS
WHEN MY MOTHER HAS NO MONEY TO GIVE.

IF YOU REALLY WANT TO BE PRODUCTIVE
YOU SHOULD FIND A WAY TO ADDRESS
THE THINGS THAT HAVE CAUSED MY FAMILY
TO BE IN THIS TERRIBLE MESS.

AND THEN YOU'D UNDERSTAND
WHY WHAT IS FIRST IN MY MIND
IS NOT THE FACT THAT IN YOUR CLASS
I KEEP GETTING BEHIND.

Chapter VI
RKN

The next letter is from a 42-year-old housewife and dance teacher. She has been in recovery for the past eight years. She wishes only to be identified with the initials RKN. (It has been interesting to see the varied ways the submitters wanted to be identified. Some specifically wanted their real names used. Others chose pseudonyms, and others only by first names.)

RKN experienced physical, emotional, spiritual, and incest abuse within her family. Her letter brings to light the sensitivity she felt with some of her teachers. Her re-traumatization within the school should awaken us to the inappropriate behaviors some teachers knowingly/unknowingly display.

Her letter is insightful. Survivors learn quickly to become, "people pleasers," especially toward men. She is confused about her own behaviors: cute and possibly flirting. (Teachers with strong and constant boundaries can defuse these situations.) RKN's laughter was not that at all; it was a reaction due to fear. Teachers need to question student reactions to teacher actions. Do they fit the situation? If not, teachers need to become aware and take notice.

Dear Mr. P,

I don't like you very much. I never really did, but I learned early in my youth to please men that I didn't like and you will be no exception.

There is something strange about you and I feel funny inside when I am near you. I have no idea why I act so cute around you, I think I am hoping that if I look cute you will leave me alone. Maybe I am flirting and don't even know it. The only thing I really know is I don't like you.

I hate the way you look at me, like you have x-ray vision and are undressing me with your eyes. I see you look at other girls that way too, and the way you joke and tease makes me feel uncomfortable, but I laugh anyway. I do that because I am scared,

scared of you, so I laugh.

I used to laugh at my uncle too. He scared me the same way, taking my clothes off with his eyes, lusting after me, slobbering kisses on my lips and trying to feel my breasts. I was 12. Now I am 14. This has been such a hard year and part of that is because of you. It is not just you though; it is Mr. S. also. Girls say to be careful because he likes to look down your blouse when he is teaching. Wouldn't be the first time that has happened to me. Mr. B. our pharmacist did that to me. I was 10. No bra yet, he saw my budding breasts right in the store. It was only a second. No one said anything, but that look stays with a person. Ten,12,14, you don't forget, the look.

I know you taught me English. I don't remember much but I got an A. I got A's in Mr. S's class too. He taught Math. Made me sit right next to him, or did I choose that seat? I watched my blouse closely. He had eyes for someone else, but not you; you had eyes for me.

I will never forget the time I came to visit you from high school. Why, why did I come see you? You swooped me up in your arms, off the ground with your arm around my back and under my legs. My short skirt did not cover my buttocks and I am sure the boy I was with saw my panties. In fact, anyone in the hall would have seen.

I was so embarrassed. I wanted to die. I hated you, but I laughed. Now I hate me.

You were an asshole Mr. Jack P., a real asshole. The students knew. Funny how the students know but the adults don't. We warn each other, but warning doesn't always help. I didn't know how to handle your flirtations. I just didn't want to get hurt, so I laughed. You don't deserve to be called a teacher. You don't deserve the position.

I have to forgive myself for laughing at your flirtatious remarks. I was young and inexperienced at saying No! I learned to please men. You were no exception.

I just want you to know - I didn't like it, I didn't like you.

RKN's confusion toward Mr. P. may bring confusion to the reader as well. Is the confusion stemming from her abuse experiences from home or does RKN have valid intuitive feelings about her teacher? Her statements of acting cute and flirting could be in the range of normal behaviors for a high school student. But, she does so with the full knowledge that she does not like Mr. P. RKN conjectures that acting cute will keep her teacher at bay. This exhibits higher level thinking skills whether they are logical or not.

RKN's feeling of being undressed by the teacher's eyes is understandable from the perspective of a sexually abused student. This is all the more reason for teachers to keep a highly professional demeanor about them. Even the slightest whimsical body or verbal language message may trigger, in an abused student, reactions that seem inappropriate.

Another teacher, Mr. S. seems to have a reputation of looking down girls' blouses. Judging what is valid or simply perceived behavior from adults to students is difficult. I reiterate that constant professional demeanor on the part of teachers will prevent possible inappropriate assumptions by students.

It was not so many years ago that I was returning from a field trip with my class. As I sat on the bus, I supervised the behavior of my students. To my consternation I observed one of my female students dressed in a loose fitting tank top. With the strong wind blowing through the bus windows, this young student's tank top billowed allowing her full-formed breasts to be openly viewed. I was concerned that the boys in the area would also notice and start an embarrassing situation for the girl. In a subtle state of shock, I sought the help of two of my female colleagues to speak with the girl about the appropriateness of her dress. I was to experience an even greater shock at the reaction of the two teachers I asked for help. Their response was, "Well John, did you get a good look!" My mouth dropped open and I stood there transfixed. What was I to say? My concern for a student's well being turned on me as a sick view of male teachers' ability to interact and respond to female student situations.

I proceeded to ask the school counselor for help in talking with the student. She did agree with me that the braless tank top dress was inappropriate for this student on a school function. This kind of situation is difficult for male teachers and needs to be addressed with professionalism and female colleague assistance.

RKN writes to another teacher:

Dear Mr. B,

You are my ninth-grade science teacher. I am in the honors class, but I don't know why. I feel so stupid, and I don't understand.

You are different than the other men teachers I have. It doesn't seem like you try to undress anyone with your eyes. I like you, but I find it difficult to concentrate. When I am not afraid of you I start to daydream.

By this time in my school career, I am so good at daydreaming I don't know how I am getting my work done. I could never come and tell you. I am supposed to be perfect and not ask questions.

It doesn't make sense to me because I ask questions of my other men teachers, but not you. I think it is because I am afraid I will like you, I could maybe even trust you, and that would be wrong. Trusting men is wrong and dangerous. It is better just to laugh and pretend you like them and stay away from them.

It really was too bad. There was so much I didn't understand. But I did like you and it is not your fault.

Take care and God bless you in your career.

RKN's low self-esteem is seen in this letter. She was placed or recommended to the honor's science class yet didn't feel she belonged there.

We become privy to some valuable knowledge about student survivors of sexual abuse: "trusting men (women) is wrong, dangerous." What a sad commentary that a student who may like the teacher needs to protect him/herself for fear of being betrayed once again.

RKN shares her confused state in this letter. She does not comprehend why she behaves in certain ways: daydreaming when relaxed, staying away from someone she may like, laughing and pretending with teachers she didn't trust.

A final letter from RKN:

Dear Teacher,

I don't know who you are, or what your name is. I don't even know if you exist, but if you did exist, then I want to tell you something. All through the years I was in school from kindergarten to eighth grade you never really knew who I was.

You see I had to pretend. I had to be perfect and so I made up a way to do that. It was my job to make you happy and getting good grades made you happy. It made my mom and dad happy too.

So I worked very hard to please you and I did. I got very good grades and at the end of the school year you gave me awards. I don't know where the awards are now. I didn't keep them because I was pretending. I was a fake.

I did everything you asked me to do, everything. I hid my pain. When things happened to embarrass me or hurt my feelings, I hid my pain. Lot's of times I nearly choked on my tears because I had to swallow them. It wasn't right to cry and people that cried in school got made fun of, plus if I cried at home I got slapped, so I couldn't let anyone see me cry, EVER! I pretended to be happy and you liked that. You liked my smile.

I pretended to be smart by asking questions, raising my hand, giving answers and doing homework and you liked that. Sometimes I was very afraid of you. Like the time I was in first grade and you were old and mean, and all dressed in black. You looked so hot in those heavy clothes and I was afraid of your rosary. You used to swing it and it scared me.

Sometimes I liked you, like in the fifth grade when you were a regular lady in regular clothes. I liked you a lot then, except for the time you slapped the palm of my hand with the ruler. I forget what we did, but you slapped the whole class. I hated you that day. The metal edges of the ruler cut my hand. I didn't cry. I swallowed my tears again. I couldn't show anyone because my mom said, "If you ever get into trouble at school, you'll get it even worse when you get home." So I didn't tell. Besides, the look in your eyes made me think the nuns made you do it. It is called corporal punishment.

That day made me really sad. I knew then I couldn't trust

anyone, not even you, my teacher. I began to look out the windows a lot. I am so glad we had windows. I would watch the squirrels in the trees and just drift away. Sometimes you caught me not paying attention so you would call on me. It put me on the spot and I got embarrassed. That made me feel very stupid. So I would try to pay attention.

The daydreaming got worse, but I learned how to hide it. I could daydream and take notes at the same time. I took good notes and then doodled in the margins. The doodling helped me daydream yet still look as though I was paying attention, at least enough to stay out of trouble.

I learned to trick you by asking questions. If I asked you questions you thought I was paying attention and then I could go back to daydreaming. I had to daydream. I didn't know how else to stay alive.

You liked my mom and dad a lot. My family was very involved in the church and school. My mother volunteered at the school and you and lots of the other teachers liked her a lot.

I had to keep pretending. I pretended so much that soon I forgot I was pretending, I stopped wanting to tell anybody, I stopped being real, except in music class. I loved music class. I liked singing, I felt real.

But even in art class I pretended. You always gave projects that had to look the same. I wasn't fun. I just copied you—more pretending.

You taught me a lot about God. You taught me that I was born with sin. You taught me that I was a sinner. You taught me that no matter what I did I was not worthy of God's love. You taught me that the only way I could get God's love was through Jesus.

You wanted me to be like you. You wanted me to be a nun. You wanted me to sacrifice my sexuality. You wanted me to marry Jesus. You wanted me to be God's bride.

I didn't know what you were talking about. I was in second grade. I didn't want to be anyone's bride, but I wanted Jesus to love me. So I wore the white dress and veil, but inside I felt funny. I pretended again. I liked my white gloves and purse. I made my first communion. I made my mother happy.

One day I came to school and something bad happened. You weren't there. No one said why. I was in third grade. You were a man. I never knew why you left. That whole year is blocked out. I don't know who came and took your place. Why did you leave? Why didn't you say goodbye? I liked you, you were a man. I never had another man teacher until I got into ninth grade. I miss my third-grade year. I wish you could help me remember.

Sometimes I wish I could come to you now and ask you if you knew my daddy was "touching" me. Sometimes I want to ask you, did you know I was daydreaming, did you know I was pretending, did you know I needed to cry?

I am sure you didn't because I had great role models for deceit, my parents. I wish I could believe that you cared, but I don't. You just wanted me to get good grades. And I did.

RKN's third letter is a composite address to many of her teachers. As with other survivors she believes her teachers didn't know who she really was. Students keeping the secret of sexual abuse feel they can never really be seen for who they are: survivors.

Unlike other survivors who struggle in school with severe distractions, RKN has skillfully used it to her academic benefit. While "pretending" she succeeds making the adults in her life happy. The poignancy of her self-awareness seems rational. She does not keep her awards as she felt they were unjustly deserved. After all she was pretending; she was a fake. This look into a young student's psyche can enlighten teachers to the complexity of students. What we are seeing on the surface is a fraction of the whole student.

The pain of RKN's early school years was great. A teacher's professional, gentle, and empathizing demeanor may help students cope better with their lives.

We are able to see the skills RKN was capable of early on in her education; being able to daydream and take notes, asking questions, and then continuing to daydream.

RKN's experience of Christian schooling probably caused her more confusion for her situation. The message of being a sinner, sacrificing one's sexuality at an early age is inappropriate for any student.

Having been sexually abused magnifies this confusion.

The concluding commentary of deceit and not trusting her teachers is sad. An educator's task is a challenging one. With abused students it becomes overwhelming. The more teachers observe and understand student behaviors, the greater the emotional intensity becomes. I believe increased education and professional support for teachers is necessary for the well being of students, teachers, counselors, administrators and the entire educational system. The sampling of letters in this book is clear evidence for this.

Chapter VII
DONNA

Donna Covello of New York was recently featured in Good House-keeping, February 1996. Her letter speaks for itself of the ultimate betrayal by a trusted adult in the teaching profession. Her abuse occurred from the ages of 14-16. She is now 36 and, "feeling a little better every day."

As professionals, we must realize that our field has members who should never be around young people. Continuing to set and keep appropriate boundaries is imperative. Teachers also must accept the awkward responsibility of keeping alert to any possible improprieties by colleagues with students. Reporting any such suspicions and/or events to trusted counselors and administrators is appropriate.

Donna's courage to come forth and confront her perpetrator is to be commended. Her letter put my stomach in knots—the knot of nausea.

Dear Teacher,

I am writing to you at this time to let you know how I really feel about you. When I saw you back in June, my stomach was in knots and my heart was rapidly beating. I felt sick. But the joke was on you. I wore a body wire tape recorder around my chest that day. As the wires and the recording devices were pinching my body, that little machine was slowly taping your sick words. That's right, your words, as you joyfully described the sex abuse you inflicted on me when I was 14 to 16 years of age. That's right, your words, as I sat across from you, you happily recounted the time you inserted objects into my vagina and anal area. That's right, your words, as your eyes became gazed you were recalling the time when you forced me to have oral sex with you and you becoming angry when I spit the semen out of my mouth. Your words, as you smiled into my face and reminded me of the urination games you forced me to play. Oh teacher, how dare you tell me that I enjoyed it all. Well guess what, I didn't enjoy it at all. I hated it. I hated when your body was on top of mine. I hated your touch, your smell, your face, your hands, everything about you I hate.

I was confused, scared and lonely. I thought what you were doing to me was loving me. But no, you were abusing me, hurting me, degrading me, humiliating me. Not loving me. Back in those days, I would have settled for anything that I thought was love, even if it hurt me. Also, teacher, your words ripped through me like a knife. That's right your disgusting words that you used to call me on a daily basis. Words like: "stupid, ugly, and dumb guinea." Dear teacher, who the hell do you think you are?

Your role as a guidance counselor was to help, support, encourage, and guide a student to be the best that they can be. What you really are is a pervert. I hate you so much.

Teacher, I had the last laugh. The secret is out, most everybody knows now. Thanks to you and your bragging words, you are in big trouble. Thank God, after all of those years, YOU ARE IN BIG TROUBLE. THANK GOD!

Chapter VIII
KAILYNE

Kailyne has been a personal acquaintance over the past four years. She is a 31-year-old social service advocate. She is in the sixth year of her recovery process from the abuse she experienced from birth until age 16. She attended school in Connecticut.

The letter below, although based in truth, was never given to any of my teachers. I did not have a teacher that helped me through the hell of abuse. I did have hope from time to time. A teacher would spark courage in me, but then it would flicker out or fade into the living room carpet—my rape scene. I was lifted from time to time by an encouraging word, or a warm embrace. Over-all, through all of my school years, my abuse droned on, but the voices found in schoolrooms faded out. This letter represents my plea for help to a seventh-grade teacher. I am glad I did not write the letter then. Not only would I have not been believed, but I would have killed myself. Any conscious awareness of my abuse would have destroyed me.

It wasn't until a college sociology class that I wrote about my abuse. The professor offered help. It was a monologue on sexual abuse. I "play-acted" a nine-year-old girl who was being sexually abused by her father. The thoughts poured out of me. The professor noted in the margins that I seemed to know what it felt like. I read most of my writings now and can see the abuse spattered on the pages in between the stanzas, a spray-painted image of hell. My hell. My writings before recovery have offered me a kind of healing. A healing that produces a rough-edged blade, but can cut through denial faster than any therapy session. I en-courage teachers to read between the lines. Writing has always expressed my pain. Most often in symbolism. But, the abuse is there. My pain is there. I don't think most children would express their abuse directly. Terror precludes this notion. I thank the teach-ers that initiated my creative writing. Indirectly they allowed my abuse to be heard. And in some sense, persuaded my suicidal spirit to rest.

The letter I present is a direct representation of abuse. It is highly improbable that these words would ever be directly expressed by a student. I have also, hopefully, interwoven some concepts that would appear in a child's writing samples, such as poetry, journal entries, and essays. Read between the lines.

Dear Teacher, dear teacher:

I am writing to you because I have died. Did you know that? I don't think you can know, because you keep calling my name during morning row call. From somewhere deep inside I respond to you. I call out my response. Some days I whisper it, some days I announce it. Can you tell the difference? It is an important clue. When I whisper my name, I am scared. I am afraid to call attention to my being. Any sudden movement may cause more pain. And I can't take any more pain. pause. I move towards you to go to my place at the blackboard. I brush by you to get your attention. You stop what you are doing once in a while and look up at me and smile. No, I scream inside of me. You don't get it, don't smile. Stand up and pull me aside. Ask me what is wrong.

If I announce my name, know that I am feeling worse than ever. If I announce my name I am purposely calling attention to myself and my changing body. My father notices too. He can see my curves and my lines now, and he says thing to me. I stand and move to the blackboard, loudly. You reprimand me for being too loud. You announce to the class that I am not being lady-like. I stare at you from a far away place. I have been a lady since diapers. I wrote you that poem last week. I told you that my daddy likes that I am a lady, and we play pretend. You smiled and told me how nice it is to have a father who loves me. Did I mention that he takes his love and puts it inside of me until I scream deep inside? pause. I go to the board and purposely give you the wrong answer, so that I can take my seat. You know I know social studies. You grade all of my tests. Doesn't it seem weird to you that I can't get one question right today?

KAILYNE

Concentrate. You tell me to concentrate. I am. I am concentrating on the pain between my legs. It makes it hard to sit down or to zip my pants. I concentrate on getting sick. The only way I know how to get out of gym class. I can't get undressed in front of everyone. My body hurts me. It is ugly and I hate it. Besides I don't know if I will be able to hide the swelling between my legs.

I begin my weekly routine of getting a stomachache. You send me on to the nurse. You express your disappointment that my attendance has been dropping. I look at you strangely. My eyes have told you every day for 100 days that I haven't gone to bed before 3 a.m. You tell me about commitment and discipline.

From where I am sitting, I am a 12-year-old mother, wife, prostitute, and porn star. I have earned my abusers more money in a month than you make in a year. I know about discipline and commitment. I am a professional, like you.

Stop. Look at me. Really look at me. Don't look away like all of my other teachers. I wrote to you because you have a caring face, and because you think girls are more than toys. You said that in class once. My ears jumped alive.

I am staring so hard at you, I can see the wall behind your head. Get busy with your assignments you tell me. I say to you with my eyes, it's already done. I finished it 10 minutes ago. I have learned how to do my homework quickly in order to escape my father's extra long stares across the dining room table.

You bring in flyers about a dance and look for a committee chair. You look at me. Everyone does. I am the one who does everything. Every committee, every class, every club. I'm the one. I am the one that is an absolute pleasure to have in class. I am the one from the perfect home. You remind me of that a lot, when I tell you in my poems that life is hard and home is bad. You write between the margins that I am lucky to have a father and mother who love me. I smile at you and agree. I move back to my seat. I sit slowly, it hurts to sit. Sometimes I sit on my feet, sometimes I stand for as long as I can. I am not being disrespectful, it just hurts.

Look at my eyes, read between the lines. I am the honor

student, the dropout, the show-off, the class-clown, and the wall-flower. I am white, black, Native American, and Asian. I am rich, poor and in-between. I am abused. Read between the lines of my life. Ask me from time to time how I feel. Ask me if I know what feelings are. Show me what feelings are. Don't turn away from what you know, what you suspect. Don't label me as deviant, over sexual, bossy, bitchy, or rude. Don't make me an adult. I am growing up, but I am still a child. I don't have the power you or anyone else gives me. I mimic my parents, my guardians. I act out my abuse every day right in front of you. Read between my life lines. I am play-acting at life. I am pretending to be 12, but I have already lived a life of a 35-year-old. I have the internal scars to prove it. Just ask me.

p.s. I have enclosed my homework assignment. You asked us to write the obituary of someone famous who has died. I don't know anyone famous, so I wrote my own:

Kailyne, age 12, died of heart complications related to her sexual abuse. She is survived by her abusers.

Kailyne's letter of self-introduction stresses the importance of written and verbal expression to allow an abused/neglected student to find hope. Her expressions helped her suicidal tendencies to subside.

Kailyne gives us a composite portrait of survivors and the behaviors they may display. Kailyne's writing is a fictional creation, based in realities. Her experience, background, and involvement in the adult recovery process brings forth the stark realities found within the letter.

Kailyne's student has died; more of the "Soul Murder" symptomology. The student gives subtle clues to the teacher in voice tones: "whispers" and then, "announcing." Do we listen to how students speak to us?

Child survivors may see our body language differently than what they are meant to be. Do we take notice of how students react to body language: smiles, frowns, postures, and voice tones? Is it an expected reaction? If what teachers observe does not equate with what they say or do, should they confront or counsel with the student? At least they might store to memory how the student reacted.

Middle school students are developing quickly in body and mind.

This is a difficult time for most students. Teachers typically allow this to explain many student behaviors. This frees them from questioning behaviors any further. Do we write behaviors off too quickly?

Student lack of concentration is common at any age these days. Do teachers accept this as a norm? Kailyne's student couldn't concentrate. Any wonder? In the KCET Video, "Healing Sexual Abuse: The Recovery Process." (1991) Hosted by Dr. Elina Gil, an adult survivor reflects back to age 8 or 9, "At the breakfast table, before school, I had to eat my cereal across from my father molester acting as if nothing happened the night before." Adding up: the lack of concentration, illnesses, refusal to dress/undress for gym, attendance, and facial expressions, are teachers looking? Can they see more clearly? I believe they can.

Kailyne's letter is difficult. Sometimes the truth is hard to address, yet we must face it. It is part of a responsibility of teaching. Aside from the job description of delivering the set curriculum in creative and varied lessons, teachers are obligated to "LOOK" at students.

What teachers say in class is heard! Kailyne's student saw a caring face and heard, "Girls are more than toys." Most severe abuse will never be seen, yet concern and caring words make a difference—they plant the necessary seeds for future healing through role modeling.

The insights continue in the letter. Schoolwork is done well and done quickly—all to avoid abusive adult reactions. How could any teacher have ever guessed why? They couldn't; however, with increased awareness and realization teachers will observe differently. Teacher actions and words will be different with this knowledge. These changes will benefit all students.

President George Bush's phrase, "A KINDER GENTLER NATION," seems appropriate for a teacher's demeanor. A NATION OF KINDER AND GENTLER TEACHERS could be a simple idea to keep in the forefront of one's personal teaching style.

Why has the teacher missed the clues in the student's poetry — even amid the words expressing a hard life and bad home? The teacher doesn't validate the student's writings. Why not? Does the teacher not want to know? Does he/she wish it weren't so? Could it be that the teacher lived a similar life and believes the student's couldn't have been as bad? If the statistics hold true, many teachers are survivors of child abuse. Whatever the reason—is it an excuse?

Sitting on one's feet is noted. I have seen this body behavior often over the past 10 years. I coined the term, "perching." (Another teacher in a graduate class came up with the identical term at the same time. We had never met. I will share credit for the term with her.) On the surface it is no big deal—I just instruct the student to sit properly and he/she does. But... what if there's more? Pain. I don't tell them to sit properly anymore. What if? They perch sometimes—so? I allow them this freedom just in case.

Kailyne concludes her collage of students by telling us to LOOK. Her conclusion is filled with imperative suggestions that any and all teachers could implement.

The poignant finality of this letter rips at my heart. Kailyne speaks of realities that just shouldn't be.

When you decide to "Look," please be sure to have a network of fellow educators with whom to share and consult. The video presentation, "PTSD in Children: Move in the Rhythm of the Child. Helping Victims of Post-Traumatic Stress Disorder." produced by Joyce Boaz of "A Gift From Within," emphasizes the concept of clinical self-care. The doctors and therapists in the presentation discuss the reality of "burn out." The fact of relentless responsibilities taking a toll on our overall health is an issue we must face. Our colleagues can be an essential part of a much-needed support system. We cannot deal with students who live with this kind of trauma alone. We need each other; we deserve each other...for our sakes as well as our students.

CHAPTER IX
ANNE HART

Anne Hart experienced trauma in her life until she was 48 years old. She has been in the recovery process for 12 years participating in 12-step programs. The past 7 years she has been doing recovery work with memories. Her school experience was in Virginia. She presently resides in Connecticut.

Dear Mrs. Giannini,

Do you remember me? I was the skinny, quiet little girl with blonde hair and scared blue eyes in the back of your third grade class. You liked me. You are the only teacher I remember until high school. I felt safe in your class and didn't leave my body. You hugged me once and I have treasured the hug ever since. You stood at recess and I stood right beside you, too scared to even play with the other kids. I remember you told me you didn't much like merry-go-rounds either. It made me feel much less peculiar, since all the other kids liked to ride on merry-go-rounds.

One day you came to our house. We lived way out in the country, and you drove 15 miles to see us. Were you worried about me? I've always wondered. I used to be sick for months at time—maybe you thought this was strange. It was. But you couldn't have imagined what was wrong, not in a million years. My mother was so sweet. My father was so handsome and strong. We looked so good on the surface. But they abused me at night in horrible ways, and then pretended it didn't happen in the day. And I had to pretend too, or the abuse would be worse the next time.

I could never even begin to explain to you what they did to me at night with their friends. But I was so grateful to you for your kindness. It was a warm home for a terrified, bewildered 9-year-old, a place to go and be safe and cared about. Your compliments on my schoolwork gave me courage and hope. You filled a place in my life that has made an enormous difference. Thank you with all my heart.

Anne's letter to Mrs. Giannini brings out the obvious importance of teacher actions both simple and great. The simple, "come natural" hug from a teacher lasted decades for Anne. The teacher compliments amid horrific home abuses planted "Everlasting Seeds" of courage and hope. The teacher also showed gentle empathy with Anne on the playground. What an act of kindness that made a great difference.

But Mrs. Giannini also chose the courageous, risk filled act of a home visit. Are these the actions of the past? Surely, Anne's parents must have become more guarded after the visit or maybe not. Monsters rarely stop out of fear; their powerful facade of denial keeps them going. Should present day teachers once again be trained to conduct home visits? Would this help protect and save our neglected and abused students? Certainly, it is a consideration. Although today, I would never suggest a teacher go alone. Our culture is just too filled with skepticism and illusions. Two professionals observing a home environment would be necessary for legitimate validations.

Anne's letter alludes to extreme abuse from masquerading parents joined in with outsiders. What terror! Anne's 9-year-old person must have thought this was a normal life, yet on some higher level she sensed something terribly wrong. Most students sense the incongruity of abuse in childhood when nurturing should be in its place.

Anne's heartfelt thanks to her teacher is a thank you to all teachers who choose to act for the child's wellbeing. All teachers should periodically take ownership for the positive, nurturing responses to students. It is valuable to one's profession to realize the effects of our simple acts.

CHAPTER X
DEBI

Debi has written a letter to her high school counselor. Her experience was of such a nurturing and positive nature that she chose for herself a vocation in counseling others recovering from abuse related dysfunction. Debi experienced traumatic abuse at the age of 8. She has been in the recovery process herself for the past 9 years. She is 30 years old and lives in Ohio.

Dear Counselor,

A day doesn't go by where your influence in my life doesn't cross my mind. Without your guidance, patience, and encouragement I don't believe I would have ever taken the path that has lead me to where I am today. I want to tell you that next month I will graduate with a master's degree. I believe that the main reason I have been able to accomplish this is because you believed in me when I was an adolescent. I can remember my adolescence being troublesome. I walked out of school and I skipped classes. I was there physically but not mentally. I barely applied myself in high school and I missed out on learning what was necessary for me to enter college and enter the work force. I can remember our long talks in your office during my study hall time and sometimes even during classes. You showed me compassion and patience and love. I felt a safety with you that I'd never felt before. You took the place of my father because my father never talked with me about my feelings or my problems. My father was unavailable emotionally. He wasn't interested in my life. But you were and you guided me. You provided that nurturance I needed from a father that I didn't get. You provided the direction I needed educationally and you instilled in me a hope and enough confidence to take the steps toward further education and an exploration of myself. I wanted to contribute and be to someone what you had become to me, a confidant, a helper.

I started at Akron University in psychology and now I'll graduate with my master's in counseling. Just like you. If you weren't in my life at that very critical period for me encouraging me and help-ing me to not give up or lose hope, I believe I would have lost hope and I wouldn't be graduating in a month. I still struggle with even some of the same issues I did back then but in a different context. But I do believe I have grown and I am very thankful toward you for showing me a way that I didn't even think was possible for me. Your encouragement has made all the difference in my life. I will always cherish and be thankful for you giving me your time and a part of yourself.

Debi's letter of grateful appreciation to her high school guidance counselor sends a message of an adult believing in an adolescent. How did Debi know her counselor believed in her as a person? Because of the time given to her in the counselor's office, Debi received what she did not get from her father: nurturing, caring, concern, and time. But what exactly was it that made such a great difference? We will never know specific details, but as with other teachers and adult caretakers, this counselor did, or said, or listened in just the right way for Debi at that time in her life.

Today, whether a child is abused or not, parent/child time is at a premium. Our culture has become so busy that many parents do not or can not find the healthy amount of time to be present to their children. Teachers are a natural source of attention for students. Some teachers refer to it as the "Velcro Effect." Students crave, demand, and are pre-pared to get adult attention in any way they can. As teachers, let us be prepared to give them the best we can; yet, it must be remembered to take care of one's self as well. Setting appropriate time boundaries to be with students will help prevent "burn out."

**In Memory of Debi
1998.**

CHAPTER XI
CASSANDRA

Cassandra is a fellow educator from Tucson, Arizona. Early in her teaching career she came to realize a need for early childhood education about abuse: "Six years ago when I began teaching, an incident occurred in our kindergarten class that helped me realize I needed to do some teaching about abuse and protecting ourselves. At this point, I was still repressing my own memories of abuse so had no concrete ideas or research about what to do with 5-year-olds. I called every resource I could find in our large city and was told no one had a program or even advice about working with young children and abuse issues—the youngest started in first grade. I was appalled because I know abuse happens to very young children as well as older. I now have what I consider a decent presentation/discussion for my children—some if which continues all year long."

Cassandra's experience and response to create a program to fill a void in early education brings the harsh reality of early childhood abuse to the forefront. The abuse of infants, toddlers, and primary school aged children exists. It is difficult for teachers to observe innocent kindergarten students and think of the possibility that an adult could perpetrate physical and/or sexual abuse against them. For the average teacher these thoughts are sheer insanity; yet, we know statistically through research and daily newspaper body counts, that the innocents can be abused very early in life.

Cassandra's letter focuses on her positive experience with one very special teacher. Her nurturing memories with this teacher go back to her very introduction into the public school system. What powerful messages through action and interested listening teachers deliver. Thirty-five some years later, Cassandra, clearly realizes the depth, strength and value of one teacher's loving concern for her student.

I have gleaned from this letter a role model for myself. Mrs. Adamson's intuitive, caring, and professional manner helped keep a child's spirit alive.

Dear Mrs. Adamson,

Your friendship to me through the years, but especially in your kindergarten class, has been a much needed source of comfort for me. You will probably never know how many children you have been important to—but I want to thank you for them and for myself.

My rape by an uncle began several years before I attended school and was so devastating to me that I repressed those memories even as it continued through the years. But as I look back on my school years what stands out for me are the teachers who really seemed to take a personal interest in me. I see myself as a child desperately searching for recognition and acceptance. I spent many recess times talking with you, my favorite teacher, and in later grades volunteering for chores, doing extra homework, making A's, and seeking my teacher's attention in many ways. These teachers who came to visit in my home, who spent time talking with me at recess, who encouraged me to show my talent and knowledge, who took time to explain hard school work, who asked me to be a special assistant to them, who encouraged me to step out of my familiar shell; these teachers helped me to feel loved and secure in a world filled with mistrust, secrecy, terror and pain.

In my healing process, when I am discouraged with the abuse still perpetrated on children, the fact that brings me the most comfort is that just one trusted, caring person in an abused child's life can mean the difference for that child. I am so fortunate that I had many people in my life to help nurture me—and I am healthier and happier because of this attention.

Your caring ways as my teacher have helped me to become a better teacher. Each year I have at least one child that I suspect is being abused when not in school. It is difficult to see 4,5, and 6-year-olds already with terribly low self-esteem, terrified of changes in their lives, acting out in inappropriate sexual ways, unable to interact well with their peers, who often need to be with me constantly. But I cling to the hope that even though I often cannot do anything to stop the abuse for the child (who is usually too terrified to disclose abuse) that my loving, caring consistency may be a link for that child to a more sane, loving world. Often it is the child who clings to me (as teacher) that reminds me of myself in school clinging to some security. It is often difficult to feel that needed, but I am reassured it will make a difference. Certainly there may be other children who suffer from abuse that react differently, but these are the ones to which I am drawn.

Thank you for your link in my life that still helps me to recover and heal from a devastating violation.

Fondly,
Cassandra

Preschool rape! That Cassandra survived to write this letter as a healthy well-adjusted adult is a miracle. Preschool rape! This fact violates every aspect of child rearing. How could a human perpetrate such a vile act? Yet, Cassandra takes us quickly into the sane, safe experiences she had at her schools; teachers taking a personal interest in a child searching for recognition and acceptance. I join Cassandra in thanking all of her teachers who saw her as a wonder-filled, lovely person.

Cassandra speaks to many teachers. Mrs. Adamson is the single recipient of accolades for many. Cassandra reiterates what many Dear Teacher writers have said, "...trusted, caring teachers in an abused child's life brings comfort."

Teachers themselves can take "comfort" in this fact.

CHAPTER XII
DIANE

G. Diane Hill is a registered nurse living in Maine. She states, "I appreciate your idea to inform teachers. I agree that this is an area of dearth. I have presented to this audience, myself, though my avenue is through public speaking. They are misinformed, ill-informed, and frightened to open a can of worms that they will need to contend with whether they are wrong or right."

I believe Diane's statement holds much truth to it. Teachers, being ill trained, have inadequate skills to want to choose to confront the suspected abuse of students. Hopefully, with additional teacher training and staff development, teachers may be more likely to respond professionally to suspected cases of child maltreatment.

Diane has produced a one-woman theatrical drama of hope, compassion, and education validating the abuse survivor's struggle for recovery. This presentation is available on video. It is titled, *"In Light We Grow."* Diane experienced trauma to the age of 14. She has been in the recovery process for six years.

Diane writes:

My school experience seems trivial, in many respects. But it wasn't trivial to me. It might have seemed trivial to teachers, because I don't think I showed signs of neglect, no bruises, I was well behaved (generally), and was a student who was able to learn.

Yet, because I was subject to ritual abuse, numbers were an issue for me. I was handicapped in learning math skills. Numbers frightened me. I could only add, subtract, multiply, divide, slowly. It was particularly frightening to me to hear the teacher call out those numbers. I would dissociate (appear to be day dreaming), and be unable to listen/hear/think. It was an advantage to me, when we'd go into higher numbers, because they did not have the same connotation to me, and I could go beyond the fear of hearing numbers, to thinking about what needed to be done. It was also an advantage to me that I was desperate to please, so

I would find ways to learn, in spite of all the internal static and emotion.

Also, while I was in grade school, when the teacher slowed down speaking for phonetics or reading, it was frightening to me. It resembled the drug induced and dissociative/partial awareness that I had heard during the abuse. It was therefore very difficult for me to gain those elementary skills. Fortunately for me, if there is a fortunate in this, I dissociated most of my trauma, too, so I knew only that I was afraid of many, many situations; I did not know why. I only thought that I was a coward and could self-talk away my day dreaming with, "You should pay attention. Don't be stupid," etc.

My teachers were confused as to why I would have crying jags. They tried to ignore me. One teacher I clearly remember saying to my parents, "When it is raining or storming out, I always know where to find Diane, she is in the cloakroom standing in the corner, crying," and she giggled as though to say, "That's just the way she is and I can't do anything with her, but she is at least likable."

My abuse included sexual and emotional abuse from my parents. They, however, appeared very friendly and supportive in public, only "strict." They were well-respected members of the community, in their work, church, and in my school. My fear was translated by them as being "well-behaved."

I remember having the fun of chasing boys in my class, getting them down, sitting on them, and laughing, telling them to kiss me, and enjoying that they seemed intimidated. I was in FIRST GRADE. Where in the world did I learn such behavior?? You guessed it. It was being done to me, labeled as "fun," and would proceed to forced oral sex. I didn't do that on the playground. I didn't have the right anatomy. I did like to turn the table of intimidation.

I remember a boy in school, sitting in a tree, and undoing his pants so that his penis would show to anyone of us on the playground (the days of unsupervised playground). I didn't tell on him. I did know that I didn't like it. I didn't know that anyone else wouldn't like it, too. One of the kids told. The boy was scolded.

He was shunned. I was surprised and pleased. I wondered, 'Why did they scold him? I didn't know that that wasn't OK. I wish other people would tell that it is not OK. (Like to my dad, like let him know that he could be shamed, too, if he kept doing it. No one told any adults other than the teacher, as far as I know. No one ever talked about it outside of school. When I told my parents what had happened at school, and what had been said the rules were, my parents were, again, quite quiet. I was disappointed. No hope there I guess.' I thought.)

Wouldn't it have been great if SOMEONE had known the signs of abuse? Wouldn't it have been great if someone had had the courage to question what was going on in my house? Wouldn't it have been great if someone had...taken me away from that house and helped me be safe. No, the environment was too contaminated. A respected neighbor was abusing me, too. Other neighbors, I know now, were sexually and physically abusive in their families. The school was filled with "normalized" abuse. A teacher would have had a tough time bucking it. She would have been called crazy. This way, I only thought I was. Everyone else was "normal."

As I read Diane's letter, a few questions came to mind that could be considered. Diane asks us, "Where in the world did I learn this behavior?" She answers, "You guessed it." This is one point of the _Dear Teacher Project_. Educators don't guess "it." Educators, in general, find many ways to explain or rationalize inappropriate student behaviors— sexual inappropriateness being one such behavior. This is not to blame teachers for not understanding, it simply points out that we need additional training and development about student reactions to experiencing sexual trauma in their lives.

Another question I would desire to research is Diane's behaviors toward other students. She found ways to intimidate her peers. This was a need for her at the time. She states that she did not sexually abuse classmates with oral sex, as she had been violated, because she did not have the anatomy. I wonder what she might have done if she did have the right anatomy. What if Diane, or countless other female students, were boys experiencing what they had survived. Would she have acted out sexually to perpetrate against peers, forcing oral sex on them as experienced at home? Continued study and research must progress so we may understand more fully what behaviors sexually traumatized children might exhibit.

Diane is not the first writer to mention difficulties with math. Her difficulty seems directly related to the experience of ritual abuse. Further research might find a direct link of math difficulties and traumatic sexual abuse.

Diane is desperate to please her teachers. This may be translated into a need to be accepted, affirmed, and receive praise. Her creative and energized self found "ways to learn." How might teacher observations relate this to the multiple intelligence theory?

Diane's experience of "drugged-like" slow, phonetic speech would be impossible to observe by a teacher. As a student, this was a dramatic reaction precipitated by the teacher's voice. This type of unfortunate experience would be impossible to prevent. Survivors of sexual abuse have a myriad of "triggers" that are hard to detect.

Teachers who choose to ignore certain student behaviors need to contemplate the wisdom of their inaction. Diane's "crying jags" were saying something to those around her. Some of her teachers chose not to listen. I wonder if they had known about the abuse if they would have acted differently?

Finally, Diane asserts that had a teacher suspected abuse and reported it, the teacher would have experienced a tough time. The teacher would have been labeled "crazy", as Diane's perpetrators were socially accepted adults within what looked to be a normal community. I understand Diane's concern. There exists a subtle atmosphere in the education field that discourages full teacher awareness and attention to abuse issues. Often, adult perpetrators of children are strong community members who have skillfully created a facade. This facade of a well-known and trusted adult is difficult to "buck." How would the community believe a teacher's observations or knowledge as opposed to a person they view as one like themselves? This whole issue is difficult for teachers to even think about. Keeping our head in the sand, remaining quiet, and choosing not to question certain student behaviors, allows maltreatment to continue unchecked.

CHAPTER XIII
ERIN

Erin is a housewife from Ohio who is active in education and speak-out programs about child sexual abuse.

Dear Sister Lucille,

I hope you still remember me, but more important I hope you'll remember what you saw.

I was the child who was always early to school. Even though we had to stay outside, in line, until the morning bell. Rain, cold, or snow I was always first in line.

I was always quiet, I never spoke unless asked, and even then I spoke so soft it was hard to hear me. My homework was always done, I got straight A's. I was always very helpful, doing whatever was asked of me. And yet, I always seemed to be dozing off. That was because either my father was in my bed, or I was afraid to go to sleep because I thought he would.

I always stayed as late after class as you'd let me. Any excuse would do. "Let me help you clean the classroom erasers...Teach me to play the guitar, please." I didn't want to go home. Sometimes you had to physically show me the door.

I was an outcast with the other children my age. I acted older than my years. I had to; I was an adult in a child's body. I was my father's mistress, my mother's counselor, and my brother's mother. I was never a child. The other children could sense this, and knew I was different. So I was never accepted. I was picked on, bullied, and ostracized. I wasn't one of them and never could be.

I asked you to help me become a nun. I know that you hear that a lot from little girls in a Catholic school. But I was more insistent than others, enough that you and Father Velarie even talked to my parents. I wanted to be a nun who was a nurse and a missionary. First, I thought if I was close to God I couldn't be hurt anymore. Second, I hoped I could die a martyr, somewhere in the jungles of Africa. That way I would be able to get to heaven, I'd be a saint. I obviously couldn't do it the regular way, I'd have to work harder to get to heaven. I was too dirty for God to even want to look at me, my dad saw to that.

I don't blame you. How could you have known? But if you had asked, it would have all come pouring out. The sex, the beatings, the neglect—all of it. Please, don't be afraid to ask! And don't be afraid of what I might say. Please Believe Me!

In Remembrance,

Erin.

Erin's clues given to her teacher begin with something that may not raise an eyebrow. Erin's early arrival at school seems innocent enough. To Erin it was an early escape from home.

Consistent academic performance and good grades probably allowed her teacher the comfort not be concerned. Erin did however tell her teacher something by sleeping in class. Many students fall asleep once in a while. This is why it is important to have multiple frames of reference for each student.

When Erin's teacher needed to show Erin the door to get her to go home, a clear message was given: I don't want to leave! This atypical behavior (early to school, sleeping in class, not wanting to leave) should have raised a suspicion at some level.

Her peers sensed Erin's stolen childhood. Why didn't her teacher sense it? If it was, why wasn't any intervention suggested?

Commonly, survivors of sexual abuse feel dirty. Erin is no exception. Internally to become clean she would have to choose a vocation as a missionary possibly leading to martyrdom.

Erin shares with us a true cost to those sexually abused as children: Death is a price to be paid to be put whole and right again. This is an extremely sad commentary.

Erin's final plea to all teachers is that we shouldn't be afraid to ask, nor to hear the response.

It is my personal belief from experience that this takes courage. To see, to ask, to listen, to hear, and to respond a teacher may be drawn into a situation that will demand much from the teacher.

CHAPTER XIV
CAROL

Carol wrote the following anecdotal experiences from her own teaching experience:

Dear Mr. Seryak,

    In an effort to be of help, to educators (I am an educator myself), I have submitted this letter. I would add that I have done a lot of reading on the subject of multiple personalities. I am not a multiple, though I seem to have many parts to my personality. Sometimes I've noticed this same thing in students.

    In my classroom experience, I have run across several children whose home life was questionable. One little girl from such a home, displayed moodiness, difficulty getting along with others—especially girls, depression, lack of consistent motivation, and extreme forgetfulness. On the latter— one day she would understand the latest math lesson completely. The next day, she had no idea how to do the same work. Sometimes she would come to school with a 20-dollar bill and give it to someone else.

    Another girl, who we were sure was being abused and who moved away when the parents were questioned—was very shy, had low self-esteem, daydreamed even in fourth grade, and was always saying she wished she was someone else. There was a problem about her not doing her homework. Her father displayed an overbearing and dominating personality in our presence. Later in the year, before they were questioned, the mother told me she had found all her papers wadded up and hidden all over her bedroom—though in school, she did not display this type of irresponsible behavior.

    At this same school, I had a little boy who had severe scars around one wrist and several fingers. In his early years, he had been tied up by abusive parents and was now in a foster home. He had low self-esteem and lack of self-discipline as well as a temper.

As a survivor myself, being with these children was probably too "triggering" for me at the stage of recovery I was in at the time. I have since transferred and do not have as many children who are at risk (as the children I mentioned).

Sincerely, Carol

P.S. — The subject of sexual abuse is not a very "happy" topic; however, I would like to state that I finally experience more good feelings than bad for the first time in my life. Attention to sexual abuse issues is important.

Carol's observations show that she is alert to student behaviors and performance. She draws no accusational conclusions from her observations. Carol does not state so, but I assume her attention and professional communications with her students made a positive difference in their lives. Healthy adults attentive to children's feelings and needs will demonstrate to children a role model who is concerned about the student's best interest. As for Carol's personal experience as a student, she writes the following:

My recovery is far from complete, but I am a survivor of sexual abuse. After years of therapy, I've had a clear memory of my mother fondling and kissing me at a very early age (2 to 3 years old). She told me that she was "practicing"—because she wanted to have more children.

During my elementary years—age 9 or 10, I went through a long period of being afraid to go to bed at night. Not just afraid— terrified. I would lie awake in a hypervigilant way. I saw "Indians" at the foot of my bed—I saw "bears" in my room. My bedroom was upstairs, shared with my younger sister, Polly. I was afraid that my parents were trying to kill me. I saw some breadcrumbs on a newspaper in the hall, and thought they were trying to lure a bear upstairs to "eat me up." (My father owned a bear coat/costume. He used to scare kids with it on. My younger cousin remembers that he crawled through a window wearing the bear costume and growling at us!) I once told Polly that I thought they were trying to kill me. I don't know what she said or thought.

Today, in my 50s and living alone—I notice that I often

"startle" right after falling asleep. It's happened so often lately, that I have been trying to recapture what I was thinking (dreaming) about before the reflex occurred. Looking back in my journal, I see that I am often on or near steps in my thoughts. Here is what I wrote:

"I take two steps (up or down—not sure) and I'm highly startled (I wake up—after just falling asleep)!! I see the pretty stairs in our house on Andalusia—they are 'really' pretty wood; I feel far less important than the steps right now. I'm up near the top of the steps. I see the pretty wood."

Because of my years, now in therapy—I tell myself whatever happened will never happen again. I picture this phrase written BOLDLY across the headboard of my bed. I tell myself that my hands are safe and that I don't have to hide them anymore when I go to bed. Still, what is that pressure I feel on the bridge of my nose? I have the feeling or thought of being on the highest ride at the amusement park—on the edge, about to fall off—and no one cares.

In a therapy session, several years ago, I experienced in imagery—a sixth-grade teacher showing empathy. In a very kind way. Mr. Ginther asked if anything was wrong—-that my grade had dropped from an A to a B (I had been a straight A student). If this truly happened, I'm sure that I responded shyly, and probably said little. I was extremely shy. In the therapist's office however— I said desperately to the teacher, "something is terribly wrong. PLEASE come over to my house—there is something sinister going on there."

Carol

Carol's sexual abuse by her mother speaks to the reality that female perpetrators do exist. Generally, the mindset of most people is that sexual abuse occurs only from males. Statistically, there are fewer female sexual offenders but new studies show they exist and are significant in number.

As a child, Carol lived in fear of her parents. Children should experience a nurturing, safe, loving environment at home. The fear of being killed by one's parents would be traumatic to a child. School must have been a place of refuge to this young girl. Carol's memory, some 40 years later, of Mr. Ginther showing concern for her shows teachers that a simple, caring comment from them makes a lasting and significant impression.

What would Mr. Ginther have done if Carol had; in fact, told him something was terribly wrong and to please come over to her house? It would take great courage and professionalism for a teacher to respond to such a challenge from a student. Educators may be faced with extremely difficult situations that do not seem to be a part of their regular job description of implementing the graded courses of study. Today's educators need to come to terms with these crucial issues. Increased staff development and structured planning for these events will help students and the whole of the school community.

CHAPTER XV
CHRIS

Chris is fairly new into her recovery process of one and a half years. She lives in Ohio and is 31 years old. Her traumatic sexual abuse occurred from age 15 to 18.

Chris' letter is very graphic and spares the reader nothing. I had a difficult time reading this letter, as should anyone. The horrors Chris experienced were, immoral, criminal, and not ethical. As this letter is read one can only ask how such a person can become a teacher and then act out with such malfeasance. This teacher was premeditatively devious toward Chris and other students. Chris' experience should send shockwaves into our educational communities. Predatory teachers like the one in Chris' letter need to be held accountable to the full extent of the law.

Dear Teacher,

You know my name! It's Chris—how could you forget?!

In my sophomore year I had you twice a day for class — second semester. First period driver's education and third period health.

I was only 16 but slowly you gained my trust. I looked up to you, I thought you were my friend.

Slowly you began touching me. I talked to my best friend about you doing this—she said you were just being friendly.

In April, you took me in a back room and rubbed your hands over my butt. Later in the month you had them down the back of my pants.

During movies in class, you put your hand on my thigh and smiled at me.

The last day of school (in my sophomore year) you hugged me in the same back room and asked me if I wanted more—I said, more what? I was very naive and innocent. I didn't know what you meant, you told me to stop by in a few weeks at school to say hi. You taught driver's ed. every summer.

CHRIS

I came by to say "Hi" and tell you I failed my Driver's test. You locked the door of the simulator. Then you hugged me and stuck your fingers up my vagina, it hurt. You told me not to tell anybody—it was our secret. I said, "okay." You told me to come back next week. You began touching me more and more. Then you took my hand one day and put it down the front of your pants on your penis. I froze. I couldn't move. I kept remembering how you told me I was special and pretty and you liked me a lot. I just stood there.

Then there was the time you masturbated on my stomach and wiped it up with your handkerchief.

Or the day in the summer in a back room of the school when you pulled down my shorts and your pants and rubbed your penis on my vagina. Then you kissed me.

The week before you stole my virginity from me you put your penis in my mouth—you had me sit in a chair—your penis began to move in my mouth it was hard to keep giving oral sex with it moving. I didn't know why it moved. I stopped sucking and you laughed at me; you rubbed my breasts a lot.

The next week (nearing the end of July) you layed me down in the simulator and raped me. You didn't say a word. I tried to push you off me at your hips but you kept going.

Later in August, after being at your house talking to you—you drove me home, stopped behind a doctor's office, took out your penis, put your hand on my neck and put it in your lap and held it there until you climaxed. I had to swallow sperm, and you were smiling. Then you took me home.

At the beginning of my junior year, the simulator became a place of sex, oral sex, demoralizing and more and more control.

In October of my junior year, you took me out in the driver's ed. car, and we smoked pot. You took me to a graveyard and had me perform oral sex on you. Then you drove me to some woods and layed me on your leather coat and had sex.

Soon after this, you told me my friends weren't really my friends; that you were my true friend. I believed you cause you had so much control over me I thought it was true, I became isolated. I only talked to you. I started taking other drugs to help me escape from all of this confusion and you. You controlled me so much.

The incident in the simulator you had me get down like a dog and you put your penis in my butt, I felt so low but you had all of the control.

Or the time you rubbed your penis over my breast. Do you know what you did to my mind? You didn't care.

I have haunting memories of you.

I also remember when you made me give you oral sex when I had my braces on—you told me not to scratch or bite you—then you put your penis down in my throat it choked me -you laughed.

At the end of my junior year, when I left my shoe in the simulator because somebody was coming in—and we jumped out the other door. It happened to be another teacher coming back there to drink on his lunch. You told me to come back a week after school was out to get my shoe. You then told me it was another teacher (you thought somebody was watching you). When I came back to get my shoe you had hidden it. When you came in the simulator, I asked you where my shoe was and you had put it in a cupboard in there. You said we were going to have sex before I could have my shoe.

Then later in the summer you called my grandma's house to have me come over and babysit your three kids while your wife was at the hospital after having your fourth child. I went to your house and none of the kids where there. I told you I was going to leave-twice. You then blocked me in front of your stairs and put your arms on the railings. You then said, "Go on up." I just looked at you then you said, "Go on." So I obeyed you. Upon entering the bedroom, you told me to take off all my clothes-you stood and watched me. When I was almost done you said you had to lock the front door real quick. You then undressed and told me to give you head.

So I did. Then the phone rang you talked to your then wife and told me to keep going. After you got off the phone, you sat on my chest put your penis in my mouth. That lasted for awhile. Then you got out a joint, and we smoked it. Then you pulled me to the edge of the bed and came. You raped me. You knew I didn't want to be there, but you made me have sex with you. I never saw you again that summer.

My senior year was finally here. It's a wonder I was still alive. I had tried suicide but failed.

You told me to join the ski club that year. Your were the chaperone. You would take me home afterwards so I could give you oral sex as you drove.

I started noticing another girl hanging around you a lot. Somebody had bought her a rose one day in the early spring that somebody was you. I asked her about you and her. She said she has sex with you. I told her about me and you. She laughed and said it was a game for you.

I had been abused sexually, mentally, emotionally by you. I was numb.

So I confronted you the next day of school. You said, "To put it bluntly, I fucked her. I love her, I don't love you."

I then said, "I loved you, why do you do this?"

You said because your wife went out on you.

That's a lie!

Then you wrote me out a pass for study hall. I was numb and shocked. Later the next day, I told a counselor about what you had done to me. He told me to forget about it-that you were just that way and not to tell my Mom and Dad. I thought there was something wrong with me because I couldn't handle it.

Two years of my life stolen from me once a week and you left me in Hell to sort out all of this damn mess.

So I buried you deep inside and tried to go on. I got married at age 21 and had a son a few days before I turned 22.

At age 26 I told our former pastor about this. He said it was my fault and told me to forget about it. He made me feel so shameful & guilty—I wanted to die again.

So I buried it again until I was 30 years old. I kept receiving prank calls for several years, so at age 30 It and God drove me into therapy. I am 32 and still in therapy.

My letter I sent to the school superintendent got you off the school system for good.

Now in the time of prosecution it will serve final justice.

I know you realize that prison shall be your home.

May you find God in the midst of your hell you chose to create.

In Christ always,
Chris.

In addition to the criminal behavior of the perpetrating teacher, Chris experienced more criminal behavior on the part of the school counselor and the pastor. Both of these professionals had a legal if not moral obligation to report Chris' story to the proper authorities.

The counselor, in particular, seems to be aiding and abetting the perpetrator. The advice Chris received was unconscionable! It would be my opinion that the counselor needs to be held professionally accountable for this advice.

The advice from the former pastor is sad, yet not surprising. As hard as it is to believe, there are frequent occurrences of inadequate spiritual direction to the survivors of sexual abuse.

As a professional educator I can only feel remorse and shame that a person in my field could act out in such a vile way. I cannot bring myself to refer to him as a colleague. My hope and desire is that justice will be served for the actions against Chris and other students.

With professional therapy and counseling, Chris does have positive opportunities to heal from this trauma.

CHAPTER XVI
DOROTHY

Dorothy of Aransas Pass, Texas introduced her letter to <u>Dear Teacher</u> follows:

Dear John,
    Thank you for the opportunity to sort my stuff through writing. What had seemed like the one sane part/place of my childhood seems after all to carry the shadow of signs of a "typical" troubled child, particularly in my teens. I didn't recognize that till I wrote the first of my "letters." I had also blocked that there were some abusers in my schools, as well as what today would be considered neglect. And gradually more memories have been drifting up, even about several years where I've had considerable amnesia. In learning that instead of a single trauma, it was the effects of compounded traumas in a single year that erased so much memory and dropped my academic ranking then. One of those events I recalled on the postscript page titled <u>Dear Teacher</u>.
    Do try to explain dissociation and how kids survive using its diversity. I tried by describing Veronica's limitations, and by stream-of-consciousness descriptions how I was "leaving" situations in seventh grade. I guess ritual abuse needs described as to the totality of its aspects.
    Sincerely,
    Dorothy.

Ritual abuse seems to be even more demanding for the common person to grasp and understand. Recently, more has been researched, studied, and written about this form of physical and sexual abuse. Ritual abuse often conjures up images in one's mind of ancient human sacrifices or satanic worship sacrifice. The difficulty with the validation of ritual abuse is the skill with which it is kept secret and covered up; however, stories like Dorothy's and others must be given credence.
    With the recent news revelations of ritual abuse coming out of

Belgium and Great Britain there is no doubt that ritual abuse does exist. As more stories are brought to light and valid investigations are documented, we will come to an understanding of the unfortunate horrors some children experience.

Dorothy addresses many teachers through her school years. She shares much that will be helpful to teachers of all levels of instruction.

An Open Letter to My Teachers:

I am a ritual abuse survivor. That means I lived thru hell. It wasn't always apparent. I hid quite well, the quiet child lost in books or standing on the sidelines. School was my sanctuary, my oasis. I was different literally there from how I was at home or where the other abusers had control over me. I tried keeping my worlds very neatly sorted for my sanity.

I only thanked two of you later. I felt embarrassed that I'd not amounted to anything significant with what you taught me. I ignored that survival matters. One of you I met when my memories had returned about the class and how I got thru it. I was so shy, saying thank you for your patience with me when I was your student. You were old, yet you recognized me and knew my name. That startled me and scared me, for it didn't feel safe that anyone would remember me after 30 years. In my heart I wanted to tell you why I almost failed the class, but I was afraid to say the words. I knew you'd never forget them. I will tell you here, later.

You never forget your first teacher. Mama brought me in a red wagon because I was still weak from the hospital, and you regarded me as an invalid. You ran a kingdom of order from your oak chair, teaching a parade of shapes that became letters and numbers, mysteries became rules; logic still evaded me. You wanted empty lines between math problems but I filled the space with countless sagas of Miss Ether Lady for several years as I drew out my year of trauma memories about the hospital. Thank you for teaching me to read boxes, old books and anything with letters anywhere. Reading was ridiculed at home, but I insisted. I was afraid of the janitor because he checked pants so I stopped going to the bathroom at school. I guess no one ever told you, or you didn't care. I wondered about that and how much you suspected about other people in the small village. Most of them had been your students once. Did you ever notice things, or was your neat world so well ordered that nothing unpretty entered?

We had a substitute teacher for three whole glorious days in fourth grade. She smiled and taught us a Dutch spinning song which I still can sing in Dutch.

The rest of fourth grade was gloomy, punctuated by the fiasco of my artwork. To bribe my way out of being beaten up by a group of boys, I did some graphic nudes and my teacher said I'd burn in hell for it. I already lived in hell, but it still bothered me. You prayed for my soul, and I felt shamed.

Fourth-grade was hard because I was distracted by fifth and sixth grades' material when I was supposed to do homework. This meant the next two years would be a breeze. Mrs. L., our new teacher, was a motherly sort who had a great acceptance for breaking the rules in the name of education so we did chemistry in inkwells and passed notes in broken French. Thank you, Mrs. L., for also paying attention when it mattered, like noting the bruises and when I came back from lunch late, crying. You noticed the homework not done, even the acid burn that you had checked at the hospital. You asked me about it over ice cream and I dared not talk because my parents would hurt me worse if I told. Thank you for trying to report the child abuse and have me taken away.

I was so scared at the time, I thought I committed a crime by being a victim, but now as an adult I understand that anywhere likely would have been better than remaining at home. Thank you so much for trying to convince teachers and the principal about the physical abuse. I am sorry Dan and grandpa intimidated the school board. You were a good teacher.

Ah, Mrs. S., the one I called a vulture because of your habit of waiting for us to do something wrong and then pouncing. Had I called you a bitch like the other kids did that day when you stepped out of the room, nothing would have happened, like nothing did when they did it. But I wanted recognition, peer popularity, and I never settled for the trite and routine, so I wrote the note and termed you a vulture, and I deserved the trouble I got for it. I'm not sure why I didn't like you. I recall so little of that year, just that episode and that something scary happened that wiped out my memory of seventh grade, and somehow I passed school, and the next year I passed state exams and graduated.

I was tense at graduation because I had got in trouble again with father. I was going to get it once the public ceremonies were over, and I did. I cry when I recall the beating and being locked in my room for more brutality and then he left, moved away suddenly. People came to help mom silence me, and they did. A month later they took me to the mental hospital and I sure fit in, and they erased my memories so I wouldn't talk. And then I moved away, so no one knew. I wonder what you knew about me, about why a bright student has so much difficulty doing homework and why my memories vanished and what happened those years I don't remember. I don't know why father moved, just that he ran and he was scared. I must have known something dangerous. And now I don't.

When I started over at the new school in the new part of the country, it was literally a fresh start for me because of my dissociative identity disorder which was very active by that age. Usually I took the same school personality with me to classes so I could remember subject matter, but in ninth grade I started to lose the continuity. This showed up with sad results in algebra class. A part of me called Veronica started showing up to learn the equations, but she only had addition skills so flunked a lot problems. Other days the part with the other math skills was there, missing important patterns of algebraic logic, so I still got problems wrong. Mrs. T. was amazingly patient with me after class, trying to figure why I could do things one day and not the next. I seemed quite spacey in class and even behaved differently, she said. I seriously tried to apply myself to this class but was making no headway. When I saw her recently, I wanted to tell her she'd had a multiple in class, but was scared to say it. The reason I'm aware of Veronica is Veronica had figured out that she was missing time but couldn't figure what it meant, only that she was incredibly dumb for an algebra student compared to the others. This kind of amnesia isn't something you confide to people, but if you notice students who are missing a lot of their marbles, it is something to consider, and definitely relates to traumas. Thank you, Mrs. T. for not humiliating me. You seemed to know I ought to be able to do the work, but you were respectful of me when I was failing class. I mattered.

My arms go numb when I think of Miss C., then I get angry. I met you first in ninth grade thru a mistake in class scheduling, and didn't have you for a class till the next year. Still, you managed to encourage me to attend art club and to meet with people who welcomed me. Being welcomed is such a strange experience. What I remember of you is very bizarre, because so much of it is dealing with nudity and sophisticated groups of adults and odd smoky places where you made fun of my shyness. I do not know how to deal with this anger at how you slipped into my life way beyond what role a teacher has and corrupted school for me. It doesn't matter to me that the same people who invaded my afterschool life also ran yours and that you probably also were victimized by them too. It's too big a hurt to me to reach compassion for you yet. I wanted my little island of safety to extend to all my classes at school, a place I could believe in pure academic interests and find friends and pretend I was like the other kids. I wanted that illusion so much, and you had no right to abuse my innocence that was left <u>even</u> if there was precious little of it left by that time. I wanted the right to that illusion. I wanted to pretend. Instead I pretended it hadn't happened, that life was just ordinary when I went to class and when you acted like a wise adult friend, I accepted that in your class I was okay. You asked my mother about me and asked me about her. You asked about my little sister. Years later, you took on my sister as an adult friend, asking my sister about me and using me as a link to her. It was so subtle, the adult stuff, so very much you leading me into your glamorous life, and I resent it, I rebel at the memories coming back about those parties at your houses. I hate what you did and weep inside for my loss. You did not have the right to use me and my sister. I can be angry now when I have the freedom to feel. I only had the moment by moment ability to survive then, not the luxury to feel.

Another hurdle of ninth grade was gym class and having to undress and shower in public (that's what it felt like). It never did feel safe and I tried all sorts of things to not have to undress. Do unmolested people have that terror? The years and situations blend in my mind. I don't remember just when Miss Y. took over and started checking when I was having my periods, but I recall the uncomfortable situation when my periods stopped and I got sent to the school nurse and everyone insisted I had to have a boyfriend to lose it. Everyone knew more about my body than I did. This calamity happened shortly before summer vacation and when I went back in the fall there was no baby. Miss Y., why was that so normal to you? Didn't anything scream out to you that a shy, quiet girl who has no boyfriends and is so inhibited doesn't just end up pregnant? Didn't anyone care? That summer my mother starved me and made me sleep with a board strapped to my belly to keep the bulge from showing. For years later, I spaced when I saw pictures of corsets with wide straps. I couldn't talk about it, I didn't have vocabulary. Doesn't anyone see the strangeness of incongruity? Doesn't anyone care at all? I have only the loneliness of remembering that I was alone then and that no one understood, not even I.

When I returned to school, I was like a different person. I wanted to start over again and I did. It is so easy to start over again and again. I have done it so much of my life.

The classes were big and so was the school so I just fell in with another group of kids and eventually things sifted out. Like Mr. H's. world history class, where they had this series of oral reports on topics. So I picked the tyrants to do my reports on, trying to understand what made them tick. God knows I had reason to try to figure out certain people I lived with. Did you, Mr. H., ever wonder what made me pick those topics?

Then there was the teacher who looked at my test results and asked why I wasn't planning to go on to college. He said my grades weren't proportionate to my potential, and was troubled. No one had said I had potential for a few years. I felt awfully guilty for failing somehow, yet I didn't believe in myself. I didn't believe there was a future beyond the day, because so much changed and depended upon my parents. I was depressed and frankly suicidal. I told him so. He said to rejoice, quoting a Bible verse.

My father used to quote Bible verses that didn't make sense too. Clearly this teacher's life was pretty different from my own. I don't know why, but I did struggle to go on to college, and I finished it. I lived. It has been hard believing myself; that goes with survivorhood, paradoxically. As I read this, I guess I made it. I do know recovery had been the most bone-chilling hard thing of my life, except for the brutal first 21 years.

To all of you who aren't my teachers from my past: please step in and save kids you suspect may be coping with massive or even mild abuse. We don't talk about it. Often we literally cannot. Today, it is easier for intervention. Today, abuse is discussed. Please believe it exists.

An important point that Dorothy makes in the beginning of her letter is that school was a "sanctuary" and an "oasis"; a safe and restful place. She tells us of her skill to separate (compartmentalize) her world at home from her world at school. Separate worlds were a necessity for her sanity. If teachers ever wonder about the abilities of students, becoming aware of the skills of survivors at such young ages should help teachers know that the human mind and spirit is capable of much.

Dorothy reveals so many insights for teachers to consider. Math, reading, art, gym all had significant effects on her in relation to being a survivor of ritual abuse. This provides good reasoning for having holistic team conferencing among teachers for the benefit of students.

Dorothy mentions her memory of the janitor checking her pants. With so many adult caregivers around children there is a need for professional demeanor on the part of all adults of any role in the schools.

Mrs. L. was one teacher who risked noticing on behalf of Dorothy. At the time these efforts failed to result in intervention with the family. Mrs. L's. action did leave a lasting impression with Dorothy. Young students know and appreciate teacher concern and action. This is important for the continued health of the education system.

There are missing pieces to Dorothy's memories as with many other survivors of sexual abuse. Her experience after eighth grade graduation is numbing. To then be hospitalized continued the trauma of ritual abuse.

Teachers are not used to considering the possibility of multiple personality students in their class; however, there have been many times in team conferences when I hear my colleagues state that a student acts or performs completely different in one setting from another. This could be a consideration in some cases. Not to rush to judgment about this possibility, but it is in fact a distinct possibility for survivors of extreme abuse and trauma. A teacher would need to consult or get advice from a professional psychiatrist or psychologist in the field of child abuse if a legitimate suspicion is warranted.

.For Dorothy's other personality, Veronica, Mrs. T. did just the right thing. Mrs. T. treated her with respect and refrained from humiliating her. Respecting the person of a student is a key message to all teachers. When teachers show respect to their students as individuals, the students know and realize this. There can be nothing more important than this in a student/teacher relationship.

Then there is the experience with Miss C. Her after—school relationships with Dorothy and her sister crossed professional boundaries. These experiences caused harm to Dorothy and left a long—term effect.

Dorothy questions why teachers didn't intervene enough over a pregnancy issue. The ineptitude of the educators in Dorothy's experience seems obvious to the reader. I wonder how much of this continues today? Sadly, I believe to some extent.

Dorothy's plea for today's educators to step in and save kids is valid. Unfortunately, I am not sure that teachers are better suited to dealing with abuse than when Dorothy attended school. There are more reports and investigations today than in the past, but I am not confident that the interventions and help are adequate for the suspected abuse of students.

Dorothy adds four specific anecdotal suggestions to teachers about her experiences as a student. These insights may be beneficial for teacher awareness and understanding.

Dear Teacher, (First grade)
Please don't ask me again if I want to be a nurse when I grow up because I draw so many pictures of them. I don't know how to stop it. See, they washed me in that big tub and then laid

me on a table with a big gas mask to make me dizzy and I woke up with this white plaster cast all over me and I couldn't get out of the crib. Those other kids, they swallowed pills like I did and then they went away and came back all changed. I'm never going to swallow pills again. They said be brave and don't cry and so I didn't. They tie up kids who cry and climb out of bed. I don't remember life before the hospital. Daddy said hurry up and walk and don't limp like a cripple. I want to please him so much. I don't remember daddy. He didn't visit me all year. He says I cost him money and I have to earn it and what am I good for. Sometimes he dives at me and I duck but I don't want to remember why, not even when he grabs my ankle again and threatens to give it a big jerk or stand me on my head. At night I dream about flying and I know I can, that you float and then you land so gentle, but people say that's silly, only birds can fly. I know I flew. Sometimes I draw people flying and put wings on them but mostly I draw nurses. I don't know why.

I was late because dad made me eat on the front porch again so people could stare at me. He hits me with the razor strap when I don't eat fast enough, both at breakfast and then at lunch when I come home to eat. If I can't eat all my food, it gets saved for the next meal. You can't eat a lot when you're scared. I am ashamed of getting in trouble for eating.

Could you please not chase us and spank us and give us a pinch to grow an inch when we have birthdays? It really scares me being chased and spanked at school, too. And my momma says it's a pain to have to make and bring treats to give to those kids who already have plenty to eat. Please don't make my momma mad.

(Seventh grade) I imagine the sound of your voice liquefied and poured slowly into the inkwell till it's a very thin soft noise far away. Your body blends into the blackboard and the marks on your dress blur with the other marks on the board, if I concentrate on it. I can make you small enough to disappear. I wish I could make Dennis and Roland disappear. They loom everywhere, warm and squirmy in their desks as you write more assignments up there.

DEAR TEACHER

I don't know why Dennis' mother said there was no room in Charlene's room for me to stay. Instead she made me sleep with Dennis and Erwin and Roland who were staying over for the night, too. And I just slid off the wall there, just turned to crud on the wall lathe and stayed safe and secure and cold, away from them. I shiver trying not to remember, and am surprised you have been speaking to me. You seem to know when I'm not paying attention and then you call on me. I don't have it done. I wasn't home yesterday. What am I going to say as my excuse why I was gone? I couldn't go home after school. There is a soft giggle from the others. They didn't go home either but it is a secret. There are so many secrets from you. You get to go home to the city when school is over. We go home here. It is different. I hate you. I envy you. You went home somewhere. Your parents didn't slam the car door and say stay out and don't come back, beg someone else to take you home. You don't understand. I can't tell you any of it. I just sit and stare out the window till you sigh and give me a longer assignment. Maybe I will do it sometime.

CHAPTER XVII
VERA

As Vera's letter is read, teachers need to ask themselves why Miss R. did nothing in response to the information she received from Vera. Vera learned quickly and well that she should not have told anyone. Telling meant losing someone important in your life. I believe this is true to a great extent even today with the constant bombardment of sexual abuse stories in the news. Many adults continue to evade the issue, minimize, or deny the issue entirely. Young people need to experience responsible action from adults they confide in.

I am an incest survivor. I hope that making people aware of the things that happened to me that no other person will have to go through what I did. If someone is being abused, I hope they will get help. I told people about my abuse and only got hurt worse.

I wish to share two events which occurred in my childhood. The two need to be presented together, in order to have a full picture.

The first being when I was 7 years old. There were two girls who lived a few houses away from me. I was restricted to certain visiting times, but was able to go on occasion. One day I was in Suzy's house. When one girl had to use the restroom, all three girls would go at the same time (three girls being myself, Suzy, and her little sister). I had no privacy boundaries anyway. That day I decided to show the girls what my "daddy" did to me at night. I told them we had to be in a dark, secret place. Suzy showed me where the crawl space to the attic was. We went into the dark area, and I demonstrated with a q-tip what my "daddy" did to me at night. He would put things in and out of both of my holes and tell me that "it feels good." The girls each took a q-tip and did the same for themselves.

A few days later, Suzy's mother came to speak with my mother. I remember the conversation clearly. Suzy's mother told my "mom" what I had shown her daughters, she said, "This is not normal behavior for a child Vera's (myself) age." My mother responded, "Well you know how kids are." Suzy's mother said that, "There is something wrong with this," and that Vera is never to play with my children again.

It was not long after that conversation Suzy's family moved away. After all who wants to live next to a child molester? As a 7-year-old I did not need someone to tell me that I was bad and that I could make bad things happen, it was my fault that Suzy moved away.

Elementary school was very difficult for me. I had no friends. I particularly hated recess. I would sit by the entrance door waiting for recess to be over. In fourth grade, this was 1972-1973, and I was 9 to 10 years old, my teacher, Miss R. befriended me. She would ask that I walk around the playground with her at recess time. I felt special that I was allowed to do this, and that Miss R. cared about me.

One day at recess I told Miss R. what my "daddy" does to me at night. I also told her that I prayed that my parents would die, but since that did not happen, I prayed that I would die so I could go to heaven. (This is remarkable considering that my parents did not believe in God, or religion.) I also asked Miss R. if I could come live with her. I do not believe I ever got that question answered.

Miss R. did not finish the school year because she was getting married and moving away. The last day I saw her, she told me to, "never forget her." Miss R. also told me, "We have a lot more in common than you will ever know," as she wiped the tears from both of our faces.

To a 9-year-old, in my eyes at that time, if I told anyone what happened I would lose them for good. No one had to tell me not to tell. I learned for myself to keep quiet.

It was about age 11, when the outright sexual abuse ended, and I started to wipe the memories out of my mind. I was 28 years old before I connected that my childhood was the reason why I was so mixed up.

In ending, I just have a few questions: 1.) Why did Suzy's mother and Miss R. not help me, or find someone to help me? 2.)

Is the same thing happening today; are people still looking the other way?

Sincerely,

Vera.

I cannot answer Vera's first question other than that it is quite possible that Miss R. was herself a survivor of child sexual abuse and felt that nothing could be done. She may have learned that from her own experience.

As to the second question, I do believe teachers continue to look the other way. That is one of the purposes of the research and concept of the <u>Dear Teacher Project</u>. Changing teacher awareness and response to abused students is imperative for a societal change to decrease child abuse and neglect.

Vera sent two poems that speak of her adult healing as a survivor:

ANGEL

She was a shining Angel hiding upon the steps.
Floating and wandering until her tormented body remains.
The radiance and innocence of the Angel shelters her from
the wickedness which nightly seizes her away.
She awakens alone in unusual places hoping to convince
herself that she did nothing wrong.
There was no compassion; her only wish that
someday she would be free from all the pain.
So very strong, surviving through all and today and adult
The She which is spoken of is ME.
I am breaking through the wall which contains my pain.
No longer will I be silent or alone, I now face my past.
My childhood dreams have come true—I have done nothing wrong.

     I AM AN ANGEL!

—Vera

SAVE THE CHILDREN

Save the children of today.
Never let one splendid moment slip away.
They are our today and our tomorrow.
Do not allow their lives to be filled with sorrow.

No one cared about me.
And I paid the fee.
Having had not childhood;
People said it was for the good.
Isn't that wild?
There IS goodness in being a child.

Protect the children of today.
Let them be free to romp and play.
We survivors must guide the way for the young.
Our work has just begun.

The children deserve better than what we had.
We were tortured; we were not bad.
We were misguided and mislead.
Leaving many wishing they were dead.
We must lead the way.
For the children of today.

Together survivors we must be strong.
Our childhoods were oh so terribly wrong.
It is up to us to change today's youth.
We must, we must STOP THE ABUSE.

—VERA

CHAPTER XVIII
LAURIE

Laurie introduced her letter to me as follows, "Mr. Seryak, I kept this short. There is so much more I could write about, but this is a letter to Jill, my gym teacher. I guess there is no embellishment for abuse."

Dear Teacher,

You abused me. You put things in my vagina such as cucumbers, wine bottles, your hand, and other things I don't care to remember. You tied me up, but that did not work well. And you were disappointed. Then when you met Robin, you cast me aside. You were done with me, the experiment was over. It was time for YOU to get on with your life, to have a family, to continue your career. You were my gym teacher, another entrusted adult, and a woman, who abused me.

It's quite ironic that all you wanted from me after all the abuse was my silence. After all the pain, silence was the least painful.

Remember that you wanted me to buy you pot? What were you thinking? I did not think, I just did. I went with you to all those places with Tom or your other boyfriends because you did not want to be alone with them. Remember, I was the kid, and you the adult. Remember that time when Tom, your boyfriend, dragged you out of the car and started to pull you into the apartment? I tried to jump on him to help you.

Another springtime graduation is approaching. The memories are clearer than they ever have been. I know that you are still married, and now have three or four kids, still teaching, yes it seems that you've gotten on with your life. Everything was always YOU.

Your Student,
Laurie.

Laurie's letter graphically validates the reality that sexual abuse is not perpetrated only by males. Her experience of gross sexual and psychological abuse at the hands of a female gym teacher is traumatic even to the reader.

Commonly and significantly, Laurie's memories are intensely revisited around the time of high school graduations. Triggers of memories around common events like graduations last a lifetime. Laurie will never be rid of the effects these memories enkindle.

To know that this teacher is still employed raises the ire within me, as it should. The insidious nature of the experience of sexual abuse confounds rational thinking. It is an effect that must be realized and dealt with. Teachers who are convicted of such criminal behavior must never be allowed in any educational system.

CHAPTER XIX
TATUM SURFACE

Tatum lives in Massachusetts and is 31 years old. She experience abuse from 4 to 16. She has been in recovery for 13 years.

Tatum sent me a short biography of her present life situation:

"I am 31-years-old. I spent my childhood years in my home with my mom and step Dad.

In adolescence, I was shuffled around from home to home.

I met my therapist at 17-years-old, I was living in a residential treatment program. My therapist worked with me for 13 intense years, she then took ill and had to terminate with me immediately.

Without her help I couldn't be where I am today.

I am high functioning. I have a dissociative disorder, I have a support therapist and a psych nurse who I check in with twice a month.

I'm married to my wonderful supportive husband Joe. I have worked many years with special needs children.

I currently feel good—finally!

The best in my life is—I am in Control and I have three <u>wonderful</u> adopted children, two who were trauma victims, one who is special needs. My children are precious gifts-I can give to them all that I didn't have. It is truly healing. Thank you for hearing my inner voice of the past-finally releasing the words I wish I could have said back then."

Tatum's recovery process shows that she is breaking the cycle of abuse. Her long years of therapy and hard inner work along with a good support network have produced positive fruits. The healing process for most survivors is a formula of professional therapy, support networking, strong family support, and creating a nurturing life. Tatum and her husband's choice to adopt is a sign a courageous healing from child sexual abuse.

DEAR TEACHER

Breaking the cycle includes creating healthy families that will pass through the educational system. The two traumatized children will benefit from this healthy family system. Positively, teachers may experience these children differently had they not been adopted.

Tatum has submitted a poem in lieu of a letter:

Dear Teacher Poem

Dear Teacher, —I have waited for this day, —To
*   begin to tell you,—Now—all that I couldn't say.*

Dear Teacher when I dragged my feet and made scuffs
*   on the floor—you yelled at me teacher and told*
*   me—you couldn't tolerate me much more.*

Oh Teacher—If you could have known—my excuse.
*   I couldn't walk right because my private parts*
*   hurt—from daddy's sexual abuse.*

Teacher forgive my spelling and my grammar too—-
*   Mommy hit me a little too hard—so I missed*
*   a lot of school.*

Teacher are you wondering—why—I didn't tell?
*   Daddy told me if I did, I would burn in hell.*

Dear Teacher you scold me—when I daydream—-
*   you ask me what i'm thinking of?—-*
*   you didn't know I was dissociating and*
*   looking down from above.*

Oh my Dear Teacher—you never asked me why
*   I was sent to a hospital for an*
*   attempted suicide.*

88

M. TATUM SURFACE

Teacher—I came to school from the
      hospital—I couldn't concentrate enough to learn.
      you Ignored me teacher, I wasn't your concern.

Oh Teacher—a Social Worker—finally came,—she
      brang me to a residential treatment center home.
      There were Kids—just like me,—that were abused.
      I finally—wasn't alone!

Teacher you thought—I was a stubborn child—-
      and there was nothing you could do.
      Oh Teacher,—Teacher,—Teacher!!!
            If you only knew!!

      —M. Tatum Surface

CHAPTER XX
HOUSE OF ANNIE

Annie requested her letter(s) be printed under the title, House of Annie, as you will come to know. She is 38 and is a survivor of Ritual abuse. She states her abuse as occurring from birth to adulthood in Iowa and Ohio. Her recovery process has been on-going for the past 22 years with on and off therapy. After misdiagnosis, Annie acknowledges her present diagnosis of Dissociative Identity Disorder (FKA Multiple Personality). She writes,

"There are so many written and/or drawn items from my school years which had hints, clues, (etc.) of what ritual abuses (trauma) I was going through, and also they go hand in hand, overlap, and help validate each other, along with existing photographs that match the essence of the recorded information. Those things combined with grade fluctuations and diary entries, proof of regressing in piano lessons during crisis times, are like a family to me. They sustain and support each other. After careful consideration, I realized one document without the other would not be as effective and copying all the material evidence would create a book in itself. Copying a few pieces would be like breaking up the family of documents.

There is much my internal system would like to say to teachers. Each Neuron Pathway (Personality) has his/her own expressions."

As you read the letters from the House of Annie you will get a glimpse of the expressions from an adult not fully integrated. Her acceptance and ownership of a number of "parts" within herself allows for different and valid experiences. The respect that each "person" of the House of Annie receives from each other is important for her functioning well being.

The House of Annie offers many insights for a teacher who may have a traumatized abused student in his/her class.

From the House of Annie
Music and Art

Music and Art classes were my favorites. They provided safe outlets for expressing my emotions. Not being allowed to have emotions at home, left a warehouse filled with expressions waiting to be released. The pieces of music I favored gave mirrored images of my inner reality. The drawings left many clues of needing to have peace, through peaceful and serene artwork. When I was younger, I was more proned to also draw the unlikable scenarios of home life.

The parents caught on to these clues being produced through art and took art away from me by age 14. Persons would ask me why I'd stopped drawing. I had been ordered to keep my mouth shut or to give the parents' recorded response, "It's not important and won't get me anywhere in life." I had made A's and B's in those subjects, won awards, and scored high in state competition. Piano lessons were taken from me by age 16 and the dream of one day becoming a concert pianist was stopped by The Parents.

The Preacher-Dad gave the high school music teacher such a hard time, she dropped me form the Madrigals, Musicals, Senior Choir, and as the accompanying pianist for the choir. To this day, there is some animosity for the parents, and also for the music teacher who buckled under the preacher-dad's criticisms. She knew some of the things I was contending with and unwittingly helped to complete a task of breaking my aspirations, which my parents had seemed to work on for years.

For me, it was the last straw, since most all of my individuality and talents had been stripped away from me. The talents had provided a safe outlet for me to feel, to live, and to have aspirations.

Along with some other adults in my life, the school counselors, some teachers and school principals had seemingly taken the easier way out for themselves and had left me at the mercy of the preacher-man and his wife. Rather than to be left to their mercy, my boyfriend and I intentionally got me pregnant, which allowed me to get married and to escape childhood.

To this day, I have contended with periodic comments from others regarding how I could have gone-on to have become a fine concert pianist or artist, with queries of why I had not pursued such. I have learned that many persons cannot comprehend the full magnitude of a child trying to survive an abusive atmosphere. Thus, in response to such persons I have learned to force a smile and to end the subject matter with, "Well, thank you for the compliments, but I chose to do other things."

House of Annie
The Admired Teachers

Charm has often felt a continued bond for her first and third-grade teachers. Words did not need to be shared, as there were intuitive feelings from these teachers, and communication shared between their eyes and mine. They heard with their hearts on "show and tell" days, when my worthlessness and abuses were masked with exaggerated, created stories of fame, fortune, and bearing witness to the horrors which "other families" were going through. The third-grade teacher tried speaking with my folks, knowing something was not right. Since dad was a preacher and well-liked, there were prepared sermons of excuses, reasons, stories and his charismatic masks waiting to be presented to those adults whose suspicions had led to confrontation. Warmth and compassion radiated from these teachers, which helped Charm learn on some level that such feelings could and did exist in the world, outside of the apathetic and abusive home environment.

From Charm.

The House of Annie speaks to us through the experience and voice of Charm. Her third-grade teacher knew something was not right. Over the years I have heard many teachers comment about a particular student, "There is something just not right here." Veteran teachers have an intuitive sense about their students from experience. When the red flag goes up teachers need to continue consistent and keen observation of a student. Documenting specific details about academic performance, personal and social behaviors, and other clues may prove valuable if needed for future reference. This is not to be used to intrusively investigate a student. Appropriate detailed observations are part of a professional educator's role as teacher.

Another thought that I have come to believe about child survivors of trauma is their ability to learn while in their experience. I have yet to meet a recovering adult survivor of sexual abuse who is not highly intelligent and expressive. When it "appears" that some students are daydreaming or not paying attention, we should understand that learning might be taking place on some level. Charm's teacher confronted a well-established and strong parental facade. Teachers who confront do what they can. Charm knew intuitively that her first and third-grade teachers "felt" for her. They were successful in their role as educators.

From the House of Annie
School Counselors...Blah!

Ricky still feels the anger and betrayal left by the eighth, ninth, and 10th-grade school counselors. "He" tried to secure prevention for the House of Annie through these well dressed, condescending, "things aren't that bad," "all families have their ups and downs," under-skilled, student helpers. When Mr. Charismatic Ego-Pumping Preacher Man-daddy was called into their offices for a shot at intervention, the Counselors egos were seduced away from what the meeting was for. They needed to have resigned right then and there. Being paid to act like you care and are supportive is a slap in the face to a victim of abuse as it is. Not doing the acting job very good and getting paid is legal robbery and emotional mind rape to the student.

From Ricky.

The House of Annie's anger is expressed well in Ricky's letter. The attempt at reaching out for help only to have the confrontation thwarted must have been excruciating for her. The pain and frustration of not being able to follow through on a process started is evident. How could this have turned out differently? We will never know.

Ricky accuses the counselors of being ill-trained and weak falling prey to the father's explanations. These are issues all educators have to prepare for. Continued training and education about parent conferences and responses to them will result in healthier outcomes. There are no easy or firm answers to individual cases. With more experience, training, and processing of parent/teacher/counselor conferences students will benefit.

Education

The House of Annie made a list of subtle and more overt clues left from Kindergarten through 10th-grade:

- Drawings of witches, cats, bloodied cats, birds, candles, circles, stars, handless persons, faces scribbled out, large eyes staring, hands tied, nude women, sexually dressed women. A person knocked to the ground with a scribbled dizzy-like tornado over the head, as other persons stood looking over the fallen person. Animals colored black or brown, so their faces were not seen.

- Writings in English provided many clues. Stories of cigarette burns, death, bathtime, chores, the good person winning out over bad person, being locked in a basement or a closet, dreams of growing up, detective stories, lists of likes and dislikes, poems of finding real love someday or not fitting in.

- Math was harder to find clues with. Except there was one very noted indication of trauma at home. My grades in Math could rise to A's and drop to F's. This perplexed Math teachers. A student must be able to focus on Math to follow the techniques. A student cannot do that when he/she is dissociated.

- History classes could be very triggering. Hearing about wars, other persons problems, persons gaining freedom, cruel leaders, witch hunts, the Crusades, our constitutional rights, and so forth, were topics that hit home inside my ongoing campaign to survive in the present day. Most of my history teachers thought that I wasn't doing my best or paying attention. They were correct. Once I obtained my freedom, I became a genealogist and found history to be quite interesting.

- Biology, and Science, were very triggering. To survive, I

had to dissociate from my body. How I dressed and how well kept I was depended on the parents' decisions, which seldom was in my favor. Being abused mentally, emotionally and physically, then attending these classes created a major internal conflict. Dissection, microscopic creepy things, reserved dead creatures, blood, and so forth, were all triggering to me. Issues and theories on evolution and the Universe was a guarantee of unending lectures from the Creationist Parents at home. My grades ranged from F's to C's. Once I was free of the abusers, I found biology and science to be interesting.

 - <u>Physical Education</u> brought out the low self-esteem, backwards, shy, vulnerable, timid, intimidated, humiliated, embarrassed, and uncoordinated aspects of myself. I hated when peers were to choose teams. It re-emphasized how well I didn't fit in. It accentuated who was popular and had self-confidence. It reinforced the negative programming the parents used on me...thus perpetuated retraumatization.

The clues that the House of Annie has shared are legitimate behaviors from students that teachers need to observe. No single clue can be taken as a suspicion of abuse, yet when teachers are alert, attentive and choose to remember the whole student they may be better prepared to deal with a possible report or intervention.

Where the House of Annie Sat

School was back in session from summer break. Quickly and cautiously I chose the desk nearest to the door, so that I could escape if necessary, or I would safely tuck myself away in the back of the classroom and by a window. I could escape into daydreaming or catch up on much needed mental and emotional refreshment. Being terrified to go to sleep at night or returning home to experience abuse, enlaced with a chilling atmosphere, kept my energy drained most of the time. Having to be hypervigilant and in defensive posturing at home left me with few options on how, when, where to get some rest.

Your teaching skills were not necessarily of poor quality,

nor was I wanting to be the student who irritated you for not applying myself, not listening, not doing as well as you believed I could, or not jumping into classroom participation. Surviving was my top priority.

By the way, you were right. I could academically do better. After I left the abusive environment, I made the President's and Dean's List in college.

From the Protector
of the House of Annie.

The Protector's choice of seat in classrooms shows an instinctual knowledge for the student's well being. Surviving is always a "top priority" of abused children. The door-outward escape, the window-inward escape and rest, were necessary for her emotional and physical health.

Gentle invitations from teachers to daydreaming students could bring them back to focus and attention allowing a survivor of abuse to rejoin the class instruction.

Grades and performance are only one indicator of intelligence. In the case of the House of Annie, the recovery process later in life proved her true ability.

CHAPTER XXI
LARRY

Larry is 60 years old and recently got divorced. He was married for over 40 years to a survivor of child sexual abuse. Larry is in private business in Ohio. He has been active the past eight years with a group for supporters of survivors of child abuse. He actively speaks out and educates the public about the legacy of child abuse. His letter may bring a different perspective to teachers.

Dear Teacher,

This letter is a recollection of living with a spouse who was sexually abused as a child by her alcoholic father and an uncle. I will attempt to relay my observations of our lives as teenagers and as an adult married couple.

My wife was a victim of childhood sexual abuse from the ages of approximately four through 12. She was the second oldest of four children and the oldest of two girls. Both her parents were alcoholics and her father was her perpetrator usually when he came home drunk and sometimes even brought friends along both male and female. When the parents' marriage was broken the children were split up into different homes. One of the homes my wife was accepted into was that of a pedophile uncle who also sexually abused her.

Growing older in this dysfunctional environment with mostly the guidance of a mother who was always in denial led her to look elsewhere for help, trust, and belonging.

I entered her life when she was just approaching her teens and I will try to reflect back into time to recall some signs that now could be clues to a major problem.

1.) Even though she has always been bright, intellectual, and interested, her ability to succeed in a classroom was negligible. In fact, even going to school let alone class was always put aside because of her low self-esteem and fear of failure.

2.) She was sexually active with several different mates

but my feelings on this was her need to belong and be loved rather than being sexual. Her morality was and is unquestionably fine. She became pregnant twice as a teenager, the second time by me. In both cases she decided to deliver the babies on her own. The first is our oldest son, the second died right after birth. This was a never forgotten tragedy in our lives and probably was the reason we eventually got married.

3.) Her demeanor during high school, in my opinion, was to find acceptance through her peers and through early sexual activity. School was never an answer because of her low self-worth, her dysfunctional and abusive family and no one to see her signs of distress and offer her help and a solution.

4.) Probably the most obvious sign that was prevalent during this time was her desire to self-destruct both suicidal and socially. If there had been more educated teachers and even if her friends had been aware of these now flagships of danger among survivors and supporters, I feel at that age she could have received help and accepted it gladly.

5.) In retrospect, her attitude as a teenager that has carried over into her adulthood has been one of opposites. She has always thought of herself as ugly when in fact she is still attractive. She thought she wasn't worthy of normal happiness and well being when we all can expect it. She acted aloof and remote when actually she was scared and confused. She feared rejection so she conceded to everyone else's needs.

I guess the more and more I learn about childhood sexual abuse the more aware I am of all the signs that were there and still are because the constant strain it has on those who are all-around the survivor. Her cries for help were always there, her low self-image, her inability to function in normal circumstances, her desire to please everyone at all costs, but especially her lack of anger and her willingness to accept blame and punish herself.

Unfortunately, the pain doesn't stop with the survivor. Childhood sexual abuse can leave its marks on the souls of all subsequent generations, and devastate the lives of all it touches including mine because it has led to separation after 40 years of support and love.

LARRY

Larry's long-term relationship with his survivor wife gives credence to observations he recalls when they both attended high school.

His partner in life was abused for close to ten years. Larry informs us that alcohol was usually involved when the perpetrator father acted out. The young girl was later sent to an equally abusive household of an uncle. What must this student have thought? How could she survive? Her life as a student would have to be low on her list of life priorities.

With no healthy, nurturing adult figures in any home the surviving student turned elsewhere. As Larry recalls, his partner placed little value in classroom achievement. Her need for love was met in varied sexual relationships. At the time it appears no one acted on behalf of a young girl in distress. Had the teachers and counselors recognized anything in her? If they had, why didn't they act? Are we any different today?

. Larry continues to say that his partner showed suicidal tendencies and obvious self-destructive behaviors. He believes better-educated teachers could have made a difference.

The behavioral and social clues to an abusive experience were many: distorted self-image, unworthiness, fear and confusion, and people pleasing. All of these traits combined should alert teachers to keener observations and concern.

Larry's final thought is a message to all educators: the scars of child abuse remain on an individual well into adulthood exacting a high price for future family members.

Professional interventions for identified abuse survivors may prevent future dysfunction in adult life. Teachers have an important role in creating situations that can prevent ongoing cycles of relived traumas.

In Memory of Larry
September 1936 – February 1998

CHAPTER XXII
SARAH

Sarah is 32 years old and living in Ohio. She has been in recovery for 11 years. She states that her trauma is ongoing.

For many survivors this is a legitimate statement. Even though the actual traumatic events may have stopped for many years the adult in recovery continues to "feel" the abuse. Often it may be the first time adults allow themselves the freedom to "feel." In childhood, they may have numbed themselves to feelings—physical and emotional.

Sarah's letter shows us an abused student who functioned "almost" perfectly.

Dear Teacher,

I was the student you loved having in your class, the one who got straight A's and never caused any problems. I was the quiet girl, the one whom you referred to on the back of report cards as "pleasant" and "nice." I was the student about whom one of you wrote, "She's so quiet, I think there might be something wrong."

There was. But I'm not sure how you could have known it unless you were paying very close attention. And my experience in school was that most teachers didn't have the time or energy to pay attention to me, which was pretty much a reflection of my life at home. I thought that if I became as perfect as possible and tried to please everyone around me and never caused any problems that I would be okay.

But I was wrong. Because though I physically survived my childhood, I have spent most of my adult life trying to find out what it feels like to be me. The problem is that when you're in an abusive or alcoholic family, you can never let anyone know what is really going on, including yourself, and the foundation of your life slowly becomes a lie. It's not necessarily lying in the sense that we usually think of it. It's not about telling a fib or making up stories. It's lying about what you feel and what you want. It's lying about who you are. What happens is that lying becomes so much a part of your life, you don't even know you're doing it anymore.

For me, the real tragedy of being abused is not the memory of what happened to me, but the feeling that the spirit of who I am has been lost. That is what I have been searching for as an adult. But there were people during my childhood, some of them teachers, who helped me stay connected to the truth, even if it was only in bits and pieces, here and there. They did it in very simple ways-by listening to me, taking me seriously, seeing beyond my quietness. I still remember those people, even today, when I feel that I have lost touch with a sense of who I am.

I think what you can do as a teacher to help the abused child-and really any child, because we all lose our spirit in some way-is to see each one for the person he/she really is. Don't encourage your students to be "good" and "nice." Don't teach them how to please other people. Tell them to be who they are, whatever that is. Give your students a place to go where they can feel and think and be whatever they want and still be accepted. That is all any of us really needs.

Sarah.

Sarah was "almost" perfect as a student. One insightful teacher suspected a possible problem. "She's so quiet, I think there might be something wrong." We do not know of Sarah's abuse, nor do we know what the teacher did or did not do to follow up on this comment, but to Sarah it was significant enough for her to remember. Sarah's admonition that teachers cannot know if something is wrong with a student unless they pay very close attention is valid. She continues, that she thought teachers didn't have time or energy to be attentive. This is sad. Teachers' lives are in fact busy and the job of teaching is exhausting; however, well-trained veteran teachers should be able to be alert, attentive, and observant of student behaviors.

Sarah states that in an abusive/alcoholic family she could not let anyone know what was going on, including herself! This is common for child survivors of abuse. This survival skill for children of not letting themselves fully realize what is going on is an important factor for survival. Later in adult years, these childhood issues can be worked out or healed through professional therapy and recovery programs.

Sarah's "real tragedy" was the feeling of losing her "spirit." This concept is covered in detail in <u>Soul Murder: The Effects of Childhood Abuse and Deprivation</u> by Shengold. There can be no greater abuse to children than to injure or "kill" the spirit of who they are! The attentive, caring teacher helps to keep the spark of a child's spirit alive.

CHAPTER XXIII
SHIRLEY

Shirley is 51-years-old living in Minnesota. Her recovery work has been ongoing for the past nine years. Her simple letter is poignant and tragic. Will teachers listen?

My name is Shirley, and I would like to tell you a little about what happened to me as a child. I was sexually abused by my parents and friends of theirs' who belonged to a cult.

They kept me locked up in a little room and I was not allowed to be with any of the other children in the family. If I didn't do what they said to do, I was beaten until bloody. I wasn't allowed to attend school often and when I was in the sixth grade I finally got the courage to tell the teacher what was happening to me. Instead of believing me, she wrote a letter to my parents. For punishment for trying to help, I was beaten more severely and taken out of school for good.

My parents told the school I was mentally retarded.

The reason I'm telling you this is because I would like to see teachers to believe when they are told by children of abuse happening to them at home. Maybe they could go to the right authorities so other children do not have to go through what I had to.

There is no excuse for what happened to Shirley. The sixth-grade teacher involved here was ill prepared and negligent. Was 1958 a time of total ignorance of childhood abuse? I think not. Historically, cases of intervention on behalf of abused children began over 100 years ago with the Society for the Prevention of Cruelty to Animals (SPCA) intervening for Mary Ellen Wilson, an abused eight-year-old. Her mother was physically abusing Mary, but there were no existing laws to protect children from parental abuse. In order to protect Mary, she had to be classified as an animal allowing her the protection under the SPCA. There were no agencies for the protection of children at that time.

Teachers must be child advocates reacting to revealed information through the proper channels and agencies. Students telling teachers of abuse must be reported to the local law enforcement officials or child service agencies.

Yes, Shirley, your letter and plea to teachers will make a difference in having them act differently than your experience.

CHAPTER XXIV
JAMES

James is a 59-year-old attorney practicing in Ohio. His letter presents us with past and present background that relates to abuse trauma. James gives us a look into the long-term effects of abuse and the price of long-term recovery efforts. His writing is frank and straightforward as many people in 12-step programs are.

Dear Mr. Seryak:

You had requested me to share with you for purposes of academic studies and writing in your field, my personal experiences of inappropriate erotic behavior in my family of origin, and the behavior that resulted from this in childhood which might alert future educators as to any problems that children in their classes might be having at home.

My grandmother had apparently become hooked on klysmaphelia, or recreational erotic enemas, a definable mental disorder enumerated in the latest DSM. This got me hooked on them, particularly since she did my toilet training until I was probably seven or eight years old. I remember how upset I became when my parents stopped this and "broke me and grandma up." I would not defecate in our bathroom in the house for awhile, but did it instead out in the woods. My mother would frequently have me help her take her brassiere off; if any further acting out ensued, I have no present memory of it. But well into my late 40s or early 50s, I fantasized intensely on having erotic relationships with these two ladies. There was also a baby sitter in the picture; I have vague memories of her toilet training, but not much else. I was treated for psychological problems caused by this dysfunctional upbringing until my mid 40s with a blanket of tranquilizers, until I got into Alcoholics Anonymous and overcame this addiction. In my late 40s I started doing CODA (Codependents Anonymous) work on the original etiology, and have sustained at least a manageable recovery. I received much counseling and have read extensively in the field.

During my public and private school career, I attended Old Trail School from kindergarten to second grade. Problems at school I no longer recall led me to attend public school at Portage Path from third to fourth, Rankin from fifth to eighth, where I had my first experience of psychological impotency, a condition which has lasted a lifetime. I attended Buchtel for high school, University of Michigan for college, and Ohio State University and the University of Akron for law school. Psychological problems in law school were so pronounced that I failed nine times in 14 years before I finally graduated and passed the bar examination. I now work with other people who have psychological problems and who have problems with the law due to their behavior. Several times during my elementary and high school years I was taken down to Miami, Florida to live alone with my mother and to go to school there. This was said to be necessary at those times because I was catching too many colds in the winters in Ohio. Needless to say, I have a lot of fantasies about those years.

There remains the question of what behavior I presented that might have called attention to my problems at the schools I was attending. I was always undersized, underweight, uncoordinated, and a subject of constant derision and harassment by other children. I excelled intellectually to gain the approval of my teachers. I developed an interest in military subjects and weaponry early on which began to intimidate my tormentors. By high school I was already in the U.S. Air Force auxiliaries which were organized to spot enemy aircraft in the event of hostilities that might be expected to occur during the Cold War, was in uniform after school, and learned to fire most individual and crew served weapons. ROTC in college and service in the Army ensued overseas. During my school years I was always a loner, with no friends. I always got notes from my parents and/or doctors to get me out of taking showers with other kids after gym class or to get out of gym classes altogether. I would use school bathrooms only if they were clear of other kids. I never slept away from home one night until I went to college and into the ROTC military womb. Following the inception of the war in southeast Asia, my family prevailed on me to leave the service to avoid my embarking on possible unauthorized missions I had considered and any war crimes that I might precipitate. I had undertaken a study of nuclear physics on my own and was working on the possibility of fabricating simple weapons systems of mass destruction. I would have successfully taken out the dikes on the Red River between Hanoi and Haiphong; I might have washed easily a quarter or more of the North Vietnamese population into the Tonkin Gulf. When I returned to civilian life, I could not handle it, and spent the following years going back and forth between law school and mental institutions. Finally, I found Alcoholics Anonymous and subsequently Codependents Anonymous and here I am now.

I wish I had more to offer you, but so many years have passed that memory is short and my tale must be brief. Hopefully some of what I have written here might be helpful to your readers somewhere down the line.

Sincerely,

James.

James' message of getting recovery help is crucial to the understanding of the long-term side effects from childhood abuse and neglect. Without the intervention of study, counseling, and the 12-step programs, James' life would be drastically different today.

In recounting his school days of intimidation and torment, James shows us a young boy alone and lost. His awkward hesitancy to use the bathroom facilities and the fabricated excuses for gym classes must have been emotionally traumatic for this young student. Many times if a student requests to use the restroom at an undesignated time, I do not object realizing they may have difficulties functioning around other students.

Raging inside, from his childhood experiences, James begins a study of tools of destruction. The knowledge of this subject seems to equalize things for James in relation to other students; they are intimidated. This anger stemming from abuse follows him into adulthood and could have led to greater dire consequences if his fantasies were realized.

James' academic success as a student probably allowed him to go unnoticed by teachers. Proficient grades may relax a teacher about other aspects of a student's life. Being a teacher means more than creating a successful academic experience. Students are emotional, psychological, social, intelligent—whole persons. I believe James was not seen as a whole person in his school environment or if he was teachers seemed not to react in a beneficial way for him.

The inner struggle and work James had to face in relation to his mother and grandmother is normal for a survivor. Abuses experienced by children are not single events. They are replayed over and over again, often for the rest of a person's life.

Teachers reading this letter may get a glimpse of the perilous results from abusing a child: life-long effects resulting in possible violent acting out, drug addictions, mental illnesses, and long-term treatments for these disorders.

I am thankful that James desired, sought out, and got the help he needs. He is another example of the recovery process and its implications.

CHAPTER XXV
CAROLYN
(formerly SR. MARY CAROLYN)

Carolyn wrote the following letter to the writers of the <u>Dear Teacher</u> letters. Carolyn has been a good friend of mine over the past 20 some years.

Dear Students,

After reading <u>Dear Teacher, If You Only Knew!</u>, I became aware of a host of feelings. I was very sad, very angry, felt very helpless. But then I realized there is something I can do. I taught for 14 years and then in a school of religion for 5 more years but this was in the years 1957-1972 and then 1973-1978. The thing I could do now is to write a letter to all my students as well as to all students in the name of their teachers to ask your forgiveness. Forgiveness for not noticing you, for not noticing the circles under your eyes, the bumps or bruises, the way it was uncomfortable for you to sit in class. I'm asking your forgiveness also for noticing things that were not necessary for me to notice as well as for those things I needed to notice and didn't. I ask your forgiveness for not smiling more, for not saying a happy word, a joyful word, and an encouraging comment that would have or could have lifted your spirit. I ask your forgiveness for not following up with your parents or for not getting you the help you really needed...for not asking you what help you needed. In the beginning years that I taught I had far too many students to notice very much. I don't write that as an excuse but as a way of saying that the system has also failed you and I ask your forgiveness for that too.

I hope and pray that those students of mine that need to read this will find it and in some way it will be an aid to their healing and wholeness and recovery.

Your teacher,
Carolyn Horvath
(Formerly Sr. Mary Carolyn).

Carolyn's letter reminds me of my own thoughts and concerns even as I teach today. As I reread the *Dear Teacher* letters I daily question myself as to how I personally relate to <u>all</u> my students. I often experience guilt, self-doubt, and regret as I recall students at risk whom I miss.

Carolyn's class sizes, and mine today, are a factor on teacher performance. Carolyn states, "I had far too many students to notice very much." Today, with additional training, teachers can observe, document, and intervene for the student's best interest; however, I have found that the number of students is a significant factor for the teacher. With class sizes of usually 25-30 students, many with special needs, teachers are emotionally overwhelmed. I find myself exhausted at the end of the day. Today teachers need to be constantly "on." That is, today's teachers' alertness and observations are mandatory. There is little time for relaxation behind one's desk. Today's students are demanding of a teacher's time and attention almost constantly. Abused students need special considerations yet so do the increasing numbers diagnosed with any number of disorders: ADD, ADHD, ODD, LD, MR, and others. Fewer students per teacher in today's classes could be a significant change in meeting student needs.

CHAPTER XXVI
MARY ANN

Mary Ann Werner is the founder of the national organization S.E.S.A.M.E. (Survivors of Educator Sexual Abuse and Misconduct Emerge.) Mary Ann's commitment to public education and awareness about teacher/administrator sexual misconduct has been exemplary. She has committed her time, talents, and financial resources to making significant changes in the professional and legal arenas for the protection of our children.

Dear Superintendent Lance,
 We've met, several years ago, just before one of our school district's board meetings. In answer to your proprietary inquiry as to who I was, I answered, "Oh, just a mother of some former students."
 I didn't ask about you. The spasms in my stomach and legs were uncontrollably ascending toward my throat. Would I scream or cry? I handed you and the others a copy of the statement I had prepared for the meeting. "The family of the victims of former teacher, L.D., request an investigation into how the report of sexual misconduct against him was handled."
 I hadn't known then that you were Myrtle Lance, L.D.'s principal, loyal supporter, and author of the letter of recommendation he carried with him as he slithered out of town.
 Myrtle, for one full year you had supervision over this teacher whom you knew to be under investigation by the state department of education for sexual exploitation of a former student. I want to talk to you about that year, as it was in your world at school, and as it was in my world here at home.
 Jim, our then 27-year-old son, had just returned from a 10-month solo bicycling trip in Europe. His self esteem and personal appearance were no better than when he'd left, head always down, an inability to make eye contact, oversized sloppy clothes, hair and beard unkempt. Communicating with him was difficult. He

was distant and withdrawn, sleeping or strumming his guitar for hours on end.

Scattered in among his meager dirty laundry were crumbled pieces of paper, one an unmailed letter. It told of Jim's involvement with his friend and former teacher, L.D, how sex had come into their relationship when Jim was a 17 year old high school junior. Other papers were notes and poems. "The enemy is within. Shut up you asshole, don't look inside. Find a safe place where you can hide." "I am friendless... at times I feel so awful I don't want to be alive." "Suppression, repression, and mostly depression, each one to be shed like different layers from a snake."

L.D. was on your special roster of mentor/teachers that year. Within days of the new term six to ten young vulnerable freshman were assigned to be L.D.'s mentees. Bonding was the intention and was encouraged. A couple of other kids wanted L.D. to be their Chess Club advisor. Contrary to school policy that everyone stay in the cafeteria during lunchtime you provided a classroom for their chess playing. L.D. addressed parents of the next year's incoming class to explain the mentoring program. So well did he exemplify the ideal mentor that he was chosen (by you?) to be the program's spokesman before the members of the school board. As my husband had recently retired from this same faculty we were friends of some of these board members. Did they know that L.D. was an alleged sexual predator? That one of his victims had been a friend of their children?

L.D. spent every day of that year in close contact with impressionable kids, in his 9th. Grade English class, as a private tutor, special mentor, and chess club advisor.

Our family circled Jim with love. He gamely reported L.D. to the state dept. of Ed. (Criminal and civil actions were not options.) Jim applied for entry-level jobs. He got a haircut and trimmed his beard. Watching his dejected body return home after each unsuccessful interview ripped the hearts out of our souls. Defeated, directionless, with no employment benefits to pay for counseling, and really no personal recognition of his need for therapy, Jim hung on.

Our younger son, Pete, cried during his call to us one day.

He tearfully told us of L.D.'s propositioning of him the day before he graduated... so bright, class president for four years... second in his class. Pete's college career ended up being an alcohol haze, as his brother's had spent in a friendless, aimless fog. My husband and I felt robbed... of the tuition monies we'd labored so hard for... and of the brilliant futures we'd envisioned for both of our sons. We cried and sighed... in isolated non-identified mourning.

Through sibling networks of rumors and confidences we heard of dozens of other close buddies of L.D.'s. Some now drugging, some outwardly 'making it', one known dead. His parents found him, a self-inflicted bullet through his beautiful 18-year-old head. His yearbook picture showed the same soft features and soulful eyes as our Jim. We clung to hope for our boys. They survived. They were alive.

L.D. surfaced hundreds of miles away. Unbelievably, he strolled into the business office were Pete was working. L.D. was seeking employment. He had your letter of recommendation with him. He asked Pete for his and our family's forgiveness. Once again Pete broke down in tears as he told us of this incredible chance event.

Jim and Pete continue to struggle each and every day to overcome the gaps in their young lives when they never told... couldn't tell. Among so much taken from them were those important young years so vital in developing social and self-confidence, ease in relationships, and self respect and love.

L.D.'s life is probably going along pretty much unaffected. Surrendering his teaching certificate doesn't present too much of a problem I'm sure. His teaching pension remains intact. There is nothing about him to alert young boys to beware...

And you, Myrtle, you're now a chief school administrator, a superintendent of one of my neighboring school districts. You attend board meetings. You're looked upon as an authority on school staff matters and on the needs of students. Has anything changed for you, Myrtle? Have you learned to be vigilant of possible L.D.'s in your school?

Myself? My stomach still spasms when I see your name or

picture in the paper. It's taken years for my legs to become firm under me again. My voice, though, has become steady and has become strong. My message now is, "Stop. Stop the denial. Educators, take accountability for the children whose lives you touch... for the good that you can do... and for the harm that you choose not to see."

When I find myself feeling old, weary, and discouraged, I remember that long year, Myrtle, how it was for you in your world in school, and how it was in my world here at home. This memory, this eternally heart wrenching memory, enables me to stand up, square my shoulders, and go on.

Mary.

Mary Ann confronts this school administrator (and all administrators) with conviction and strength. In a recent conversation with Mary Ann, she related to me how difficult it was for her to recall these past events and put her thoughts, beliefs, and feelings on paper. She continues to live with the tragic events that so altered the lives of her sons. Still, she is not selfish about her cause. Even though her own sons were the victims of teacher sexual misconduct, Mary Ann speaks for all victims of educator misconduct.

Mary Ann has no use for "kid gloves" when confronting individuals, organizations, or communities in regard to teacher sexual misconduct/child sexual abuse. She has devoted much of her life to work for change in a system that all too frequently minimizes, denies, or "whitewashes" cases of sexual abuse. Hers is not a work of revenge or vindictiveness. I hear in her voice and read in her writing a "call" to make a difference. Her organization works and lobbies for legislative change at local, state, and federal levels. This is exemplary. This is courageous. This is the "right thing to do."

Teacher sexual misconduct must not only NOT be tolerated, it must be prevented. Prevention strategies include: professional investigations in teacher misconduct cases, pre-service college-level education, proper nation-wide screening of potential teachers, and a keen awareness and self-monitoring in line with the NEA established **"Code of Ethics of the Education Profession."** (I was embarrassed and amazed that every educator I talked with, from primary to college level, was unaware of this code's existence - including myself.) The code does not implicitly speak of teacher sexual misconduct. It does however, state, "the educator - Shall not use professional relationships with students for private advantage." I propose that this code be displayed in every school building in the U.S. Teachers knowing, understanding, and being responsive to such a code can only help us all be more professional.

Superintendent Lance is not afforded an opportunity to respond to Mary Ann in this format. I would certainly welcome an opportunity to speak with her personally about her perception in regard to L.D.'s case. Dialogue and constructive, confrontational debate needs to develop within the educational institution. This book, however, is primarily a tool to be used to create awareness that will, in turn, spur on dialogue and debate.

The knowledge of what administrators know about their staff and when they know it must continue to hold them accountable. Ultimately, each local school board is responsible for the safety of all students. Administrators are agents of the school board and therefore are also responsible for student safety. Employed certified staff must hold and meet the highest possible standards of the education profession. It is the role of the administration and thus the school board to validate that each educator holds to the highest professional standards. Becoming aware, keeping alert and attentive are learned skills that must be practiced and implemented in the evaluative process with regard to teacher demeanor and performance.

The United States Department of Education has a wealth of resource materials available for all school boards and administrators. One such document is, **"Office of Civil Rights; Sexual Harassment Guidance; Harassment of Students by School Employees, Other Students, or Third Parties; Notice."** This is an excellent resource for administrators to use to help create prevention and investigation policies and strategies. With the Internet as a tool, there is no reason any school district should not be aware of and educated in child sexual abuse issues and ramifications.

S.E.S.A.M.E. is an essential, pro-active resource for all educational institutions. Preventing, confronting, and being accountable for teacher sexual misconduct is a responsibility for every educator.

A copy of the NEA code is in the reference section.

CHAPTER XXVII
LA TONYA

LaTonya writes from Indiana. She is a 34 year-old African American who experienced sexual abuse for 2 years from the ages of 15-17. She heard about *The Dear Teacher Project* while working on her masters degree in counseling. *Dear Teacher, If You Only Knew!* was a recommended reading. She wrote to me, "For so long I felt as though no one could understand what I went through. Your book showed me that there were many who did no matter what ethnicity or gender. For that, I thank you. I have put my memories and feelings to paper in hopes that others may gain some insight into the often lonely and misunderstood world of abuse."

Dear Teacher:

I wish you had noticed what was going on with me. Even if you did, I don't know how much good it would have done. You see, my abuser is a fellow colleague of yours. He's won numerous teaching awards and everyone thinks he's great. I however, know that there's a different side to him for you see my abuser in not only a teacher but he's a part of my family... my father.

From the 9th. Grade until my senior year in high school I had to endure constant sexual abuse. There were days when I came to school wishing someone would notice me. You see, I'm the girl who had an A average in most of her classes during the 9th. Grade year but as I went into 10th. Grade my grades suddenly went to a C average. None of you seemed to notice that my grades had slipped drastically. Oh, a few of you did but you just contributed the change to me having difficulty adjusting to high school (7th. - 9th. was jr. high school.) But answer me this, why did it take me so long to adjust?

As time went on, it became increasingly difficult for me to concentrate. The once outgoing, inquisitive student became introverted and could care less about math or social studies. Instead, I became more concerned with when it was going to happen again. I often missed or just didn't turn in assignments. I just didn't care! Oh! Many of you thought it was a good idea to tell my father (he taught at the same high school I attended) when I did this. Let me say thank you to those who did. On those occasions when you told, the abuse seemed to be only worse. I didn't just get his sick version of love but I was also the recipient of his expansive vocabulary. I guess my father thought he was teaching me a lesson.

You know, I don't know if I could have trusted you anyway. I know that there are some of you who know even today but I see no change in your association with him. My own uncle who happened to be personnel director of the school district at the time did nothing either. Yes, I know that, that's his brother but guess what, he's an educator too. Shouldn't he have been concerned about me and of course the safety of other students? I guess not... blood is still thicker than water.

Daydreaming became a way for me to cope. Many times when you thought I was in your class, I was miles away. Pretending that I was a different person in another place and time became my coping mechanism at home and at school. It was only because of this daydreaming that I was able to survive. You see, if I was a different person, then I didn't have to feel the abuse, the other person did. Why didn't you say anything to me about the daydreaming? I know you had to have noticed or maybe it's just that I wish that you had.

Guess what? Though you never noticed the signs, I still survived. It hasn't been easy but I'm here and I'm a survivor. Am I angry that you didn't notice? Yes, someone should have. If you had, I probably wouldn't have had to endure the abuse for as long as I did. You don't know how it felt to be too scared to tell because you had your head pushed under your bath water as a threat not to tell. You don't know how it felt to be afraid of being alone with your father, knowing that the minute your mother walked out the door that he's going to send your brother outside and lock him out. Do I totally blame you for what happened? No, there are others who should have noticed the signs and didn't. Let me again say, maybe if you did, I wouldn't have had to endure the abuse for so

long. Maybe you could have been the key to others noticing the signs. Oh well, I still survived.
—LaTonya

LaTonya points out that her father/teacher/abuser was an award winning popular teacher. This is often the case with teachers or administrators who have been convicted of sexual misconduct. Cases in which the child/adolescent molester is popular causes a unique confusion for the victim, the school, and the community. Generally, we would like to believe that child sex offenders are back street stalkers lurking in the shadows. This is not the case. Most offenders are known and usually liked by the victims. One way that perpetrators set up their victims is to lure them into a friendly trusting relationship. For LaTonya, her father had this relationship already in place. As a responsible and esteemed educator, he created an environment to prey on his daughter.

LaTonya's grades dropped dramatically when her sexual abuse experience began. It is too easy for many educators to explain and rationalize this with the explanation of adjusting to change. Certainly, students may experience grade fluctuations with change of environment, social relationships, and physical development, but teachers need to be attuned to varied possibilities. Had LaTonya shown adjustment difficulties before?

LaTonya exhibited personality changes as well. She described herself as outgoing and inquisitive and then becoming introverted and apathetic. She remembers using the skill of daydreaming to help her survive her situation. Teachers should be able to observe and document this along with a student's academic performance. Team conferences with other teachers can help support one teacher's observations with those of another. If more than one teacher suspects abnormal behavior or changes within a student, then a better case can be made to confront the situation.

In LaTonya's experience, however, we have the added complication of the offender being a teacher and her father. Who could ever imagine a situation as this? Unfortunately, this is where we are. As educators we must be alert to our suspicions and take the needed course of action. Yet, when some teachers did talk to LaTonya's father about their concerns the abuse increased. Still, this is what we must do: observe, document, and confront by reporting our suspicions using the proper reporting mandates. Maybe things would have been different if teachers had followed up with the school's administration.

LaTonya is a survivor. She wishes her abuse could have been stopped. It was not. Her letter is a plea for today's teachers to be more alert and professional in their duties in this regard. We all have a lot of work to do to provide for the safety and well being of our students.

LaTonya shares with us a poem she wrote to further express herself:

"I'm A Survivor?"

So many people say I'm a survivor... even I say I'm a survivor, but did I really survive?

Did I really survive? I don't know. There are days when I think I did. There are days when I'm damn sure I didn't.

Like when the fear immobilizes my body so that I just can't get out of bed. Like the days when I cry and cry and cry to the point that I don't think I'll ever stop. Like nights when I can't sleep... too afraid that I'll wake up and see that everything that is good in my life is gone and replaced with everything that was bad from the past.

Did I really survive? I really don't know. My husband often says that I have all this potential... I don't see it. If things were different, if I hadn't gone through the abuse, would I see the potential that he sees? Would I be this outgoing, assertive, fear nothing person that I would like to be? Or, would I still be this introverted, sometimes unsure, fear-a lot-of-things person that I am today? I feel like a shell of a person.

Did I really survive? Did I just because I'm not a prostitute, drug addict, or commit suicide... did I? Don't get me wrong, I know that I'm blessed to have not gone down that road but did I really get the lesser of two evils? Sometimes, I don't think so.

Did I really survive? Well, part of me did survive but part of me didn't.

Maybe that's the part of me that didn't need to survive. I don't know. Maybe if it did, I wouldn't be where I am today... a functioning wife, mother, and overall good person. Maybe, just maybe I did survive. Then again, maybe I didn't because there are times when I feel like I've lost **me** *but I don't know what that me was like... leaving me sad and empty. Or, are those feelings, one of loneliness... longing for that part of me that I never got a chance to know. Grieving for that part of me that will never be.*

Did **I** *really survive?*

CHAPTER XXVIII
SHARON

Sharon is 49 and experienced abuse for 8 years from the ages of 8-16. She has been in the recovery process for 5 years. She lives in Ohio.

Sharon's letter is probably one of the more challenging letters for me as an educator. As you read her letter, you may experience the same frustration I did. Sharon's story challenges me to look and observe where I normally would have no concern. As Sharon confronts educators, I find that I lose more of my innocence and am tempted to become more jaded to this issue. Yet, her insistence to challenge teachers to be less rigorous in their expectations gives me pause.

Dear Teacher,

I am sure you remember me. I was the brightest student in your class that year. You never had anything but the highest praise for me, for my work. That both felt good and awful at the same time. You see, you didn't realize that my drive to "perform" for you was really a cry for help. I had no choice (in my mind) but to excel. You see, I figured if I were good enough, or smart enough, or clever enough, maybe the obscenities that were taking place at home would end. Surely it must have been my fault. In retrospect, I realize that none of those things are true. The obscenities were going to continue regardless of my goodness, intelligence or cleverness. And it was not my fault. As an eight-year-old, I knew none of that.

It's difficult to be angry with you. Why would you "look" for "trouble" from "such a wonderful child from a terrific family." The fact that my father was the pastor of a local church only made the possibility of abuse that much more remote in your eyes. And it made my desperation more complete. Who would listen to me? Who would believe me? And the fact that the way I "acted out" was to outperform everyone else in the class further complicated the diagnosis of my situation.

I just want you to know that the signs were there regardless of what it looked like given only a cursory glance. It was more than just natural ability that drove me. It was a compulsion that far exceeded talented ambition. And it followed me well into my adult life. I was old beyond my years in your fourth grade class; you praised me for my "maturity." I was desperate to be perfect hoping it would end the madness; you applauded my persistence and dedication.

What did I want and need from you? Would it have been so difficult to make your classroom a place where I felt safe enough to stumble, to make a mistake, to "stub my toe"? Perhaps if I had had the freedom to be less than perfect, I could have experienced being loved despite that "imperfection." Maybe that would have given me enough courage to share with you what felt like the deepest "flaw" of all, the abuse I was suffering on a regular basis.

Sharon S.

How do we observe the needs in our perfect students? Not only was Sharon the "perfect" student, her father was the pastor of the local church. As she acknowledges, teachers probably did not see a need to look past Sharon's academic performance and home environment. Yet, there are definite clues within Sharon's letter that might have caused a teacher to have some concern.

Students who exhibit perfectionist tendencies are dealing with some personal or environmental factors. These factors may well be normal and within the developmental range of the individual student. However, teachers need to see the whole student. Sharon wishes some of her teachers would have provided an environment for less than perfect expectations. I have found myself doing just that in my classroom. I try to give my students permission to be less than perfect; especially the ones who are driven to succeed. Our youth have whole lives to lead and education is just one aspect of many in those lives.

Sharon also mentions her "maturity." Teachers need to be alert to students who exhibit age appropriate development "beyond their years." This could be a sign that a child may not be developing within his/her normal range. Again, this may be quite normal for the individual, yet should be observed and documented if there is cause for concern.

Sharon shares with us the wisdom that if we can accept imperfection, children may have the courage to express and ask that their needs be met. Teachers, being an integral part of a student's life, may provide the freedom for this to happen.

CHAPTER XXIX
ANNE MARIE

Anne Marie writes from New York. Her abuse experience occurred in New Hampshire when she was 5, 13, and 16 years of age. She is 36 years old and has been in recovery for 2 years. Anne Marie's content and style of writing shows remarkable insight and courage for having been in recovery for such a short period of time. There is much to learn from the following letter.

Dear Teacher,

In all likelihood you have seen children in your classroom that you suspected had been or were sexually abused. In my experience as middle school guidance counselor I spoke with many teachers who came to me frustrated because they believed a child was being abused and they felt there was nothing they could do. In many cases I shared the same frustrations. We want to save the children, and in most cases we can't. I would like to suggest something we can all do. We can work to help every child find his or her voice. It may sound insignificant, but survivors of sexual often learn that their feelings are meaningless. Changing this false belief can help a survivor begin to heal. Encouraging children and adolescents to find their voice can be scary. There are many children we would honestly rather not hear from or who are already talking more than we would like. They may be the very children who desperately need to be truly heard.

I am a survivor of childhood sexual abuse. Three different men molested me over the course of my childhood and adolescence. At 36 I have only begun to heal. I believe the key to my healing has been finding my voice. My voice was taken away repeatedly, whenever someone touched me without asking me what I wanted. One abuser told me I liked what was happening, that I wanted to be touched. I knew I didn't want it, yet I believed him. I believed he knew me better than I knew myself. It was easier to accept that I wanted what was happening than to accept that someone I trusted was capable of such behavior. Since my feelings didn't matter to him, they must not matter at all. I learned to ignore how I felt about the abuse until I didn't feel at all. Survivors often have trouble separating themselves from the people around them. This was true for me. I adopted other people's feelings as my own. It was a way to keep from being rejected. My feelings were being ignored, but if I took on someone else's feelings, I would be accepted, even though it wasn't really me who was being accepted. In essence, I disappeared and became what everyone else wanted. I lost my voice and my sense of self.

Through therapy I have discovered that I have my own feelings separate from everyone else's. I have learned that paying attention to those feelings shows me who I am. I remember one day early in therapy telling myself that I am a person separate from everyone else. It was very hard for me to believe. And I am a professional counselor. I understood all these concepts on an intellectual level, but internalizing them was another matter. Discovering that I have my own feelings has been like discovering that I am alive. Learning to listen to my feelings, and to believe that they are valid, helped me discover that I have value as a person regardless of my role in the lives of others.

I believe it is truly unsafe for some children to feel everything that is happening to them. Often they have to lock things away in order to survive. But by finding a way to express the feelings that are safe, I believe they might learn the beginnings of believing that they have value and a right to be heard. If we can help children to hold onto their own voices at least in some areas of their life, I believe they will be started on the road to healing.

I had two contrasting experiences with teachers when I was a junior high school student that I think demonstrate the role teachers can play. One experience was with a male Social Studies teacher that I had been looking forward to having as my teacher. My brother had him before me and loved him. I was thrilled to get him. Unfortunately, all I remember about him now is one comment he made to my mother. He told her I was always seeking his attention and that I had men wrapped around my little finger. I remember feeling devastated by his comment. I desperately wanted him to like me; now he had rejected me. And if I had men wrapped around my little finger, I must control them and what they do to me. In my professional role, I can understand this teacher's frustration. I have felt the same frustration with students that continually appeared at my door. But I wonder what would have happened if anyone had tried to understand the reason for my behavior rather than just criticizing it. I wonder, if he had talked to me about me seeming to need his attention, if he had tried to work out a way for me to get attention from him in a more appropriate manner, if maybe then I would have learned that there was nothing wrong with my need. I might have even learned that I deserved to have my needs met and that there are appropriate and inappropriate ways for that to happen. Instead he reinforced my belief that I was a bad person and that my feelings were meaningless. Fortunately, I had a very positive experience in junior high as well. I had two English teachers who actively encouraged all of us to explore who we were and to express ourselves. My seventh grade teacher assigned a project for us to create that represented ourselves. I don't remember the structure of the assignment. I just remember what I made: a three-sided object made from colored paper that was held together with macramé. I had a symbolic meaning for everything on that object: the colors, the pictures drawn, the words used, and the knots that made the macramé. I don't remember what anything meant now, but I remember the feeling I had creating it. My feelings and opinions about myself mattered. This teacher wanted to know about me. I loved finding interesting ways to convey who I was. My mother was critical of this teacher that talked about dreams and images instead of English, but I remember the safety to express myself. That teacher, along with my next English teacher, also encouraged me to write poetry. In my poetry I found my voice, at least for a time. And in recently returning to writing poetry I have found its healing value. As those two teachers valued my writing, they valued me. I had to find my value all over again as an adult, but I believe the start they gave me in valuing my writing eased the process.

Below is a poem I wrote in eighth grade. Writing a poem about spirit must have been one of our assignments because there were many poems on the topic (including this one) in our school's literary magazine.

My Spirit

My spirit is a rock being pushed on shore by a wave
And then washed back out to sea.

My spirit is a small plant trying to push through the earth's crust
Then being trampled by people.

My spirit is a bright shining sun
Being blocked by clouds.

When I discovered this poem as an adult I was amazed that I seemed to have such self-knowledge, and that I dared to express it. The year that I wrote this poem I remember a Science teacher asking me why I smiled all the time. I didn't know what to tell him. I believe now that I smiled because I believed that was the only way to be accepted. This poem shows that although I was hiding behind a smile, I had some idea of what was happening to my sense of self. It is comforting for me to know that my voice was not always missing. On the other hand, I'm disappointed that I don't remember anyone saying anything to me about the feelings expressed in this poem. In my experience as a guidance counselor, I have seen many similar poems written in middle school English classes. Teachers would bring to me the most upsetting poems, usually thoughts about death. I know that many, many students are carrying around a great deal of pain. Teachers and schools cannot respond individually to each expression. However, I believe children benefit whenever they find a safe place to feel and express themselves and whenever what they are saying is valued.

Helping children find their voice doesn't have to be limited to English classes and writing assignments. Children have opinions about everything. Encourage children to discover their own opinions, not the opinions of their friends, and not the opinions they believe you want them to have. Value their opinions. Help them explore where their opinions come from. You can't force a child to think and feel for themselves, but with your encouragement and respect, some just might feel safe enough to dare. And each time they manage to hear their own voices they are taking one step closer to wholeness. You may feel you are fighting a losing battle. Each step you manage to provide may be matched by ten steps in the wrong direction as soon as the school day is over. But each step still needs to be taken. You may not be able to stop what's happening outside of school, but you can still make a difference in a child's life, one step at a time. Help them find their voices. Help them dare to live.

With Support and Gratitude,

Anne Marie Johnson.

Anne's primary assertion is for teachers to learn to help students "find his or her voice." She acknowledges that this can be a scary process for some children. Often it is just the children we do not want to hear from that need to be nurtured into appropriate ways to express themselves. I am certain that any veteran teacher will be able to identify with an experience involving such a student. Knowing and understanding a child's need to "find their voice" may help teachers to become more patient, tolerant, and respectful with regard to some of their students.

Anne Marie tells us she lost her sense of self. When adults experience this due to many of life's circumstances, it is very difficult to deal and work with this issue. Often a healthy adult will seek out professional counseling or therapy to help them regain a sense of purpose and self. For a child to experience this loss of self in the developmental years of life creates significant and challenging issues. Without parental or professional help, the child will experience confusion and self-doubt that will lead to dysfunction in their social, academic, and personal lives.

Anne Marie shares with us the insights she was able to gain through the adult therapeutic process. She discovered that she was "alive." Listening to and believing that her feelings were valid created a new self-confidence that led to her "new life." Teachers can help children by validating the feelings they express. This is different from judging the child's feelings. Simply by acknowledging the existence of feelings in a nonjudgmental manner will help the child own them and be ok with the experience.

"I believe it is truly unsafe for some children to feel everything that is happening to them." I would agree with Anne Marie's assertion. Many children know that certain touch is wrong. Many of those students have been instructed to tell if they experience inappropriate touch. But children who are traumatized by a sexual assault become disoriented and confused about what really happened. Teachers who help students express themselves and instill in them their right to be heard will plant seeds for future healing. Most victims of child sexual abuse will not have the opportunity to heal from their experiences until they reach adulthood. Adults remember times of encouragement from their childhood. Sometimes these experiences help them to know that there is a healthy way of living.

Often I feel I am fighting the "losing battle" Anne Marie mentions in her closing paragraph. Her advice to teachers gives me heart to go on. By valuing student feelings and opinions with encouragement and respect, teachers will make a difference in children's lives - one step at a time.

CHAPTER XXX
JOHN: EPILOGUE

Dear Teacher,

If you are reading this, you have read further than many other teachers. In the past 2 years since the first release of Dear Teacher, many teachers have told me that they were not able to finish reading this book because it is "just too graphic" or it is "just too painful." I am neither discouraged by this nor disheartened. I understand. The courageous and frank stories written here are indeed graphic and painful. As I initially read some of them, it might have taken me days to finish reading even one letter. I often became angry, frustrated, nauseous, and then had to come back to the letter later. I understand the mentality of a teacher or anyone else who does not want to put themselves through the experience of reading such tragic and real accounts of children who were sexually abused. Actually, these reader reactions are a high compliment to the writers. The poignant honesty of the writers' voices hit home... hit the heart and mind of the reader. The pain resulting for the reader is necessary to create the awareness of child sexual abuse that may one day save the life of a child. To choose not to read the Dear Teacher stories due to the graphic details that cause pain in a reader is very understandable, but it is no excuse.

I must continue to encourage educators and childcare workers to look at the pain in some children. It is only in seeing the pain, loneliness, and betrayal in children that we will have the courage to care enough to react and do something about the epidemic of child sexual abuse not only in our country but globally as well. What if the world would have continued not to look at the holocaust, or the AIDS epidemic, or the massacres of Kosovo and elsewhere? Our ignorance, blindness, apathy, and inaction will only contribute to the prevalence of sexual abuse, as that is just what sexual perpetrators are counting on. When there is a lack of awareness and a lack of alertness to children being sexually abused, then the sexual perpetrator will have free reign to stalk his/her prey.

As professional educators we have a moral, ethical, and legal obligation to be well informed about the issues and ramifications of child sexual abuse. Our interest in child advocacy and protection coupled with respect and dignity for children will send a clear message to sexual predators that their actions will not be tolerated.

Sadly, in the past 2 years I have not seen any clear evidence of a decrease in the incidence of the sexual abuse of children. With the significant increase in media coverage and education programs children are still being sexually violated at an alarming rate. On an even more disconcerting note, I have been discouraged and angered by the number of cases involving educator sexual misconduct. Schools must be a place of safety for every student. It is the role and responsibility of every educator to provide this safe environment - physically, emotionally, and academically.

As I pen my final words to educators, childcare workers, or anyone else reading this book, I would leave you with the following thoughts:

— Every child has a right to learn in a safe and nurturing environment.
— Every child has the right to be treated with dignity and respect.
— Every child has the right to develop age appropriately in mind, body, and spirit.
— Every educator has the responsibility to provide for a safe and nurturing learning environment.
— Every educator must treat children with dignity and respect.
— Every educator has the responsibility to be aware of signs or symptoms of sexual abuse through continued professional development programs.
— Every educator is responsible for observing, recording, and reporting behaviors or performances that signal suspicions of abuse or neglect.

You could add to this list from your own experience and perspectives. I hope that you do. I encourage you to remember what you have read in these pages so that the voices of the past may help you to see the faces of today - the faces of sexually abused children. If you would like to share your thoughts, ideas, or opinions with me you may write to the address below:

John M. Seryak
c/o The Dear Teacher Project, P.O. Box 11, Bath, OH 44210-0011

ADDITIONAL READING

American Association of University Women Educational Foundation, (1993). Hostile hallways: The AAUW survey on sexual harassment in american schools. (Study No. 923012). Washington, DC: AAUW Educational Foundation.

Armsworth, M. W., & Holaday, M. (1993). The effects of psychological trauma on children and adolescents. Journal of Counseling & Development, 72(1), 49-54.

Bettleheim, B. (1989). The uses of enchantment. New York: Random House.

Boaz J. (Producer) & Ochberg, F.M. (Host). (1995). PTSD in children: Move in the rhythm of the child. Camden, ME: Gift from within.

dePerardinis, D. S. The lasting scars of sexual abuse: How to help adult survivors. Tucson, AZ: Carondelet Management Institute.

Devlin, B. K., & Reynolds, E. (1994). What types of injury suggest that a child has been physically abused? When should you suspect sexual abuse? The answers to these questions will help guide you through a nursing assessment challenge. American Journal of Nursing, 94(3), 26-31.

Frye, B. (1990). Art and multiple personality disorder: an expressive framework for occupational therapy. The American Journal of Occupational Therapy, 44, 1013-1021.

Goldman, S. J., D'Angelo, E. J., DeMaso, D. R., & Mezzacappa, E. (1992). Physical and sexual abuse histories among children with borderline personality disorder. American Journal of Psychiatry, 149(12), 1723-1726.

Goleman, D. (Jan/Feb,1992). Wounds that never heal: how trauma changes your brain. Psychology Today, 62-66,88.

Gootman, M. E. (1993). Reaching and teaching abused children. Childhood Education, 70(1), 15-19.

Hibbard, R. A., & Hartman, G. L. (1992). Behavioral problems in alleged sexual abuse victims. Child Abuse & Neglect, 16, 755-762.

Hoffman, R. (1996). Half the House. New York, NY: Harcourt Brace.

Hunter, M. (1990). Abused Boys: The Forgotten Victims of Sexual Abuse. New York, NY: Ballantine Books.

Johnson, K. (1989). Trauma in the lives of children. Alameda, CA: Hunter House Inc.

Kepler, V. (1984). One In Four: Handling Child Sexual Abuse – What Every Professional Should Know. Mansfield, OH: Social Interest Press, Inc.

Krugman, R. D., (1991). Physical Indicators of child sexual abuse. In A. Tasman & S. M. Goldfinger (Eds.), American Psychiatric Press Review of Psychiatry,10. Alexandria, VA: American Psychiatric Press.

Leehan, J. (1989). Pastoral care for survivors of family abuse. Louisville, KY: Westminster/John Knox Press.

Lewis, F. (Editor), Ravitz, J. (Director), & Gil, E. (Host). (1991). Healing sexual abuse: The recovery process.[Video]. Los Angeles, CA: Lifeguides.

Monteleone, J. (1998). Child Abuse: A Parent's & Teaher's Handbook on Identifying and Preventing. St. Louis, Missouri: G.W. Medical Publishing Inc.

The National Resource Center on Child Sexual Abuse, (1994). Teacher's kit on child sexual abuse prevention and identification. Huntsville, AL: Author.

Ohio Department of Human Services/Office of Compliance and Review, (1992). Child abuse and neglect. Columbus, OH: Author.

Paxton, C. (1991). A bridge to healing: Responding to disclosures of childhood sexual abuse. Health Values, 15(5), 49-55.

Perry, B.D. (1995). Children, youth and violence: Searching for solutions. New York: The Guilford Press.

Pipher, M. (1994). Reviving Ophelia: Saving the Selves of Adolescent Girls. New York, NY: Ballantine Books.

Polese, C. (1994). Resilient readers: Children's literature in the lives of abuse survivors. School Library Journal,40(3), 156-157.

Robins, S. (1995). They Do Remember: A Story of Soul Survival. Lake Forest, CA: Home Office Publishing.

Russell, D. E. H. (1986). The secret trauma: Incest in the lives of girls and women. New York: Basic Books.

Sgroi, S. M. (1982). Handbook of clinical intervention in child sexual abuse. Washington, DC: Lexington Books.

Shengold, L. (1989). Soul murder: The effects of childhood abuse and deprivation. New York: Fawcett Columbine.

Shapiro, A. (Producer), & Winfrey, O. (Host). (1992) Scared silent: Ways to save our children from abuse and neglect.

Terr, L. (1990). Too scared to cry: How trauma affects children...and ultimately all of us. New York: Basic Books.

Tower, C. C. (1992). <u>The role of educators in the prevention and treatment of child abuse and neglect.</u> Contract No. HHS-105-88-1702). Washington DC: National Center on Child Abuse and Neglect.

FOR MORE INFORMATION
ABOUT CHILD SEXUAL ABUSE ISSUES:

There is a wealth of information in bookstores, libraries and of course the Internet on the topic of child sexual abuse. The Internet provides a myriad of resources simply by typing in "Child Sexual Abuse Prevention." I do recommend caution when using the Internet resources, as one cannot always assume that each site is sponsored by a valid organization.

Below are organizations that I am personally familiar with:

Broken Hearts Foundation
PO Box 2864
North Canton, OH 44720

Gift From Within
#1 Lily Pond Dr.
Camden, ME 04843

The Healing Woman
PO Box 3038
Moss Beach, CA 94038

MASA (Mothers Against Sexual Abuse)
503 + Myrtle Ave.
Suite 9
Monrovia, CA 91016

National Center for Missing & Exploited Children
2101 Wilson Boulevard, Suite 550
Arlington, VA 22201-3052

National Clearinghouse on Child Sexual Abuse and Neglect
PO Box 1182
Washington, DC 20013

The National Resource Center On Child Sexual Abuse
2204 Whitesburg Drive, Suite 200
Huntsville, AL 35801
SESAME
Survivors of Educator Sexual Abuse & Misconduct Emerge
681 Rt. 7A
Copake, NY 12616

Voices In Action
PO Box 148309
Chicago, IL 60614

Youth Change
C/o Ruth Herman Wells
275 N. Third St.
Woodburn, Or 97071

Code of Ethics of the Education Profession

Preamble

*The educator, believing in the worth and dignity of each human be-
ing, recognizes the supreme importance of the pursuit of truth, devotion
to excellence, and the nurture of the democratic principles. Essential to
these goals is the protection of freedom to learn and to teach and the
guarantee of equal educational opportunity for all. The educator ac-
cepts the responsibility to adhere to the highest ethical standards.*

*The educator recognizes the magnitude of the responsibility inherent
in the teaching process. The desire for the respect and confidence of
one's colleagues, of students, of parents, and of the members of the community provides the incentive to attain and maintain the highest possible
degree of ethical conduct. The Code of Ethics of the Education Profession indicates the aspiration of all educators and provides standards by
which to judge conduct.*

*The remedies specified by the NEA and/or its affiliates for the viola-
tion of any provision of this Code shall be exclusive and no such provision shall be enforceable in any form other than the one specifically
designated by the NEA or its affiliates.*

PRINCIPLE I
Commitment to the Student

The educator strives to help each student realize his or her potential as a
worthy and effective member of society. The educator therefore works
to stimulate the spirit of inquiry, the acquisition of knowledge and understanding, and the thoughtful formulation of worthy goals.
In fulfillment of the obligation to the student, the educator—

1. Shall not unreasonably restrain the student from independent action in the pursuit of learning.
2. Shall not unreasonably deny the student's access to varying points
   of view.
3. Shall not deliberately suppress or distort subject matter relevant to
   the student's progress.
4. Shall make reasonable effort to protect the student from conditions
   harmful to learning or to health and safety.

5. Shall not intentionally expose the student to embarrassment or disparagement.
6. Shall not on the basis of race, color, creed, sex, national origin, marital status, political or religious beliefs, family, social or cultural background, or sexual orientation, unfairly—
   a. Exclude any student from participation in any program
   b. Deny benefits to any student
   c. Grant any advantage to any student
7. Shall not use professional relationships with students for private advantage.
8. Shall not disclose information about students obtained in the course of professional service unless disclosure serves a compelling professional purpose or is required by law.

PRINCIPLE II
Commitment to the Profession

The education profession is vested by the public with a trust and responsibility requiring the highest ideals of professional service.

In the belief that the quality of the services of the education profession directly influences the nation and its citizens, the educator shall exert every effort to raise professional standards, to promote a climate that encourages the exercise of professional judgment, to achieve conditions that attract persons worthy of the trust to careers in education, and to assist in preventing the practice of the profession by unqualified persons.

In fulfillment of the obligation to the profession, the educator—
1. Shall not in an application for a professional position deliberately make a false statement or fail to disclose a material fact related to competency and qualifications.
2. Shall not misrepresent his/her professional qualifications.
3. Shall not assist any entry into the profession of a person known to be unqualified in respect to character, education, or other relevant attribute.
4. Shall not knowingly make a false statement concerning the qualifications of a candidate for a professional position.

138

5. Shall not assist a noneducator in the unauthorized practice of teaching.
6. Shall not disclose information about colleagues obtained in the course of professional service unless disclosure serves a compelling professional purpose or is required by law.
7. Shall not knowingly make false or malicious statements about a colleague.
8. Shall not accept any gratuity, gift, or favor that might impair or appear to influence professional decisions or action.

— Adopted by the NEA 1975 Representative Assembly